GRAPHIC BIOGRAPHIES

Jackie ROBINSON
Baseball's Great Pioneer

by Jason Glaser
illustrated by Bob Lentz

Consultant:
James L. Gates Jr., Library Director
National Baseball Hall of Fame and Museum
Cooperstown, New York

Capstone
press

Mankato, Minnesota

Graphic Library is published by Capstone Press,
151 Good Counsel Drive, P.O. Box 669, Mankato, Minnesota 56002.
www.capstonepress.com

Printed in the United States of America in Stevens Point, Wisconsin.
022010
005705R

Library of Congress Cataloging-in-Publication Data
Glaser, Jason.
Jackie Robinson, baseball's great pioneer / by Jason Glaser; illustrated by Bob Lentz.
p. cm.—(Graphic library. Graphic biographies)
Summary: "In graphic novel format, tells the life story of Jackie Robinson and his pro baseball career"—Provided by publisher.
Includes bibliographical references and index.
ISBN-13: 978-0-7368-4633-2 (hardcover)
ISBN-10: 0-7368-4633-6 (hardcover)
ISBN-13: 978-0-7368-6197-7 (softcover pbk.)
ISBN-10: 0-7368-6197-1 (softcover pbk.)
1. Robinson, Jackie, 1919–1972—Juvenile literature. 2. Baseball players—United States—Biography—Juvenile literature. I. Lentz, Bob, ill. II. Title. III. Series.
GV865.R6G53 2006
796.357'092—dc22 2005003345

Art Director and Designer
Bob Lentz

Editor
Tom Adamson

Editor's note: Direct quotations from primary sources are indicated by a yellow background.

Direct quotations appear on the following pages:
Pages 11, 25, quoted in *Great Time Coming* by David Falkner (New York: Simon and Schuster, 1995).
Pages 13, 17, 20, 22, 26, from *I Never Had It Made* by Jackie Robinson (New York: HarperCollins, 1995).
Page 18, from *Wait Till Next Year* by Carl T. Rowan with Jackie Robinson (New York: Random House, 1960).

Table of Contents

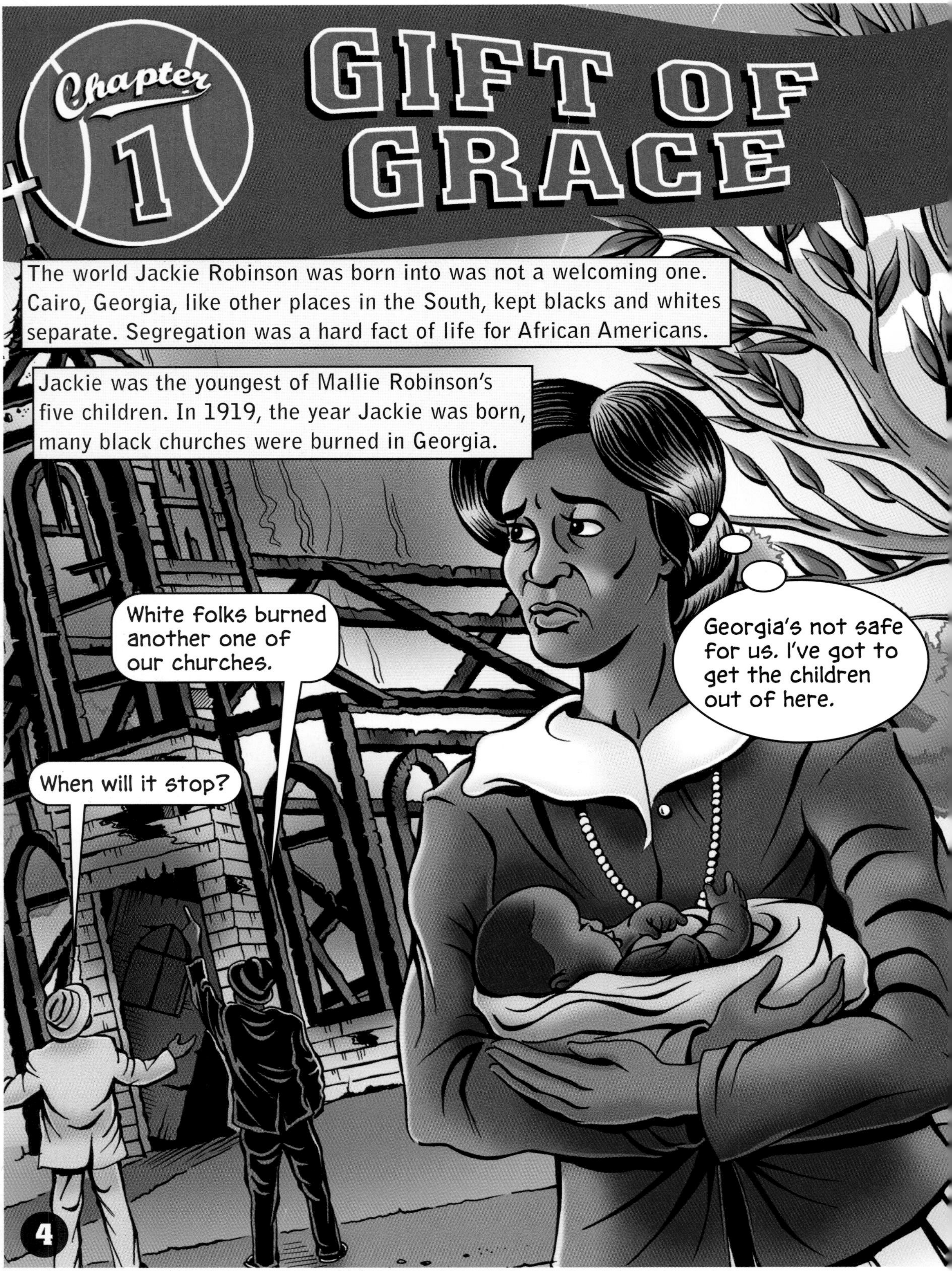
Chapter 1
GIFT OF GRACE
The world Jackie Robinson was born into was not a welcoming one. Cairo, Georgia, like other places in the South, kept blacks and whites separate. Segregation was a hard fact of life for African Americans.
Jackie was the youngest of Mallie Robinson's five children. In 1919, the year Jackie was born, many black churches were burned in Georgia.
White folks burned another one of our churches.
When will it stop?
Georgia's not safe for us. I've got to get the children out of here.

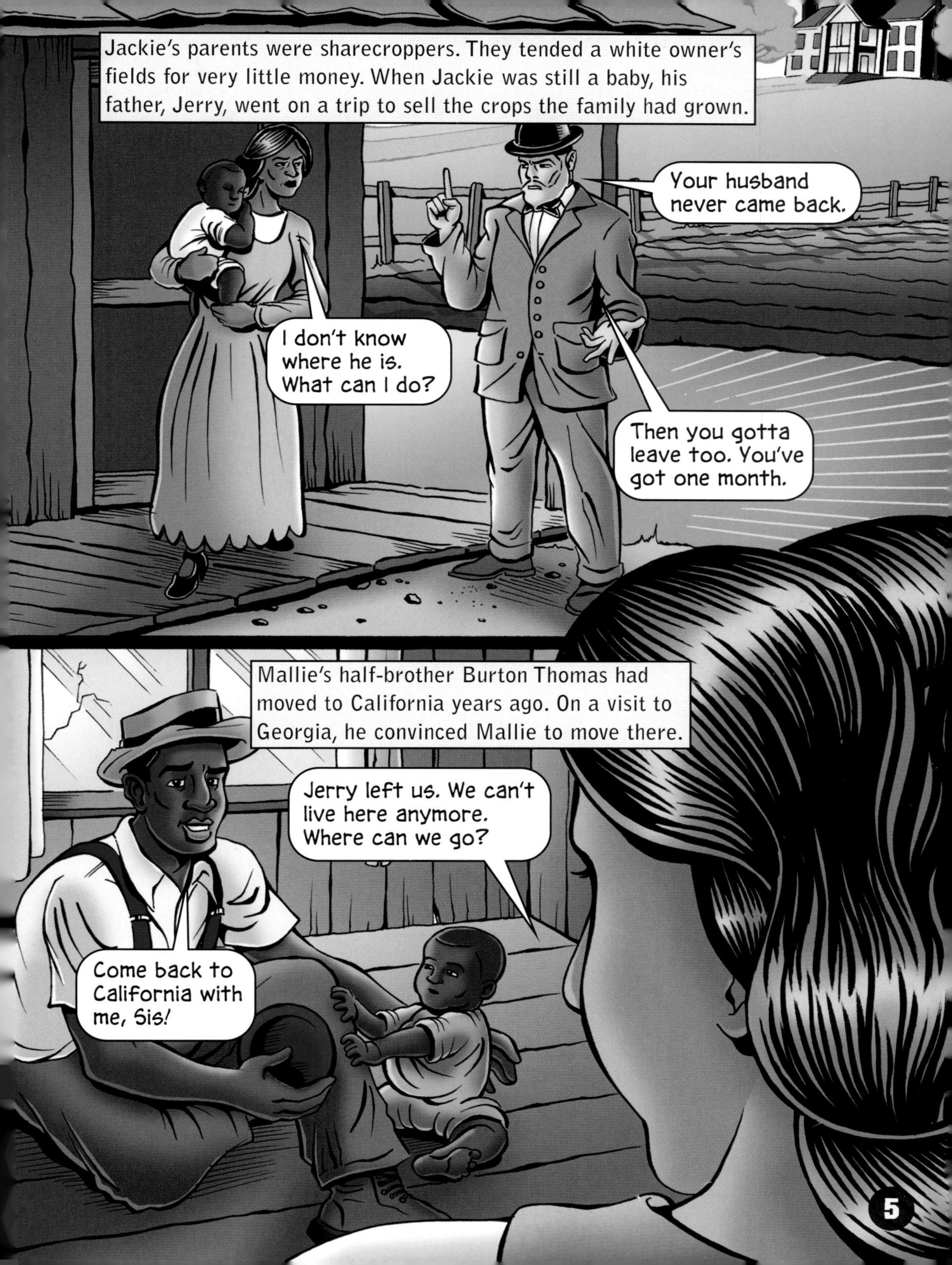
Jackie's parents were sharecroppers. They tended a white owner's fields for very little money. When Jackie was still a baby, his father, Jerry, went on a trip to sell the crops the family had grown.
Your husband never came back.
I don't know where he is. What can I do?
Then you gotta leave too. You've got one month.
Mallie's half-brother Burton Thomas had moved to California years ago. On a visit to Georgia, he convinced Mallie to move there.
Jerry left us. We can't live here anymore. Where can we go?
Come back to California with me, Sis!

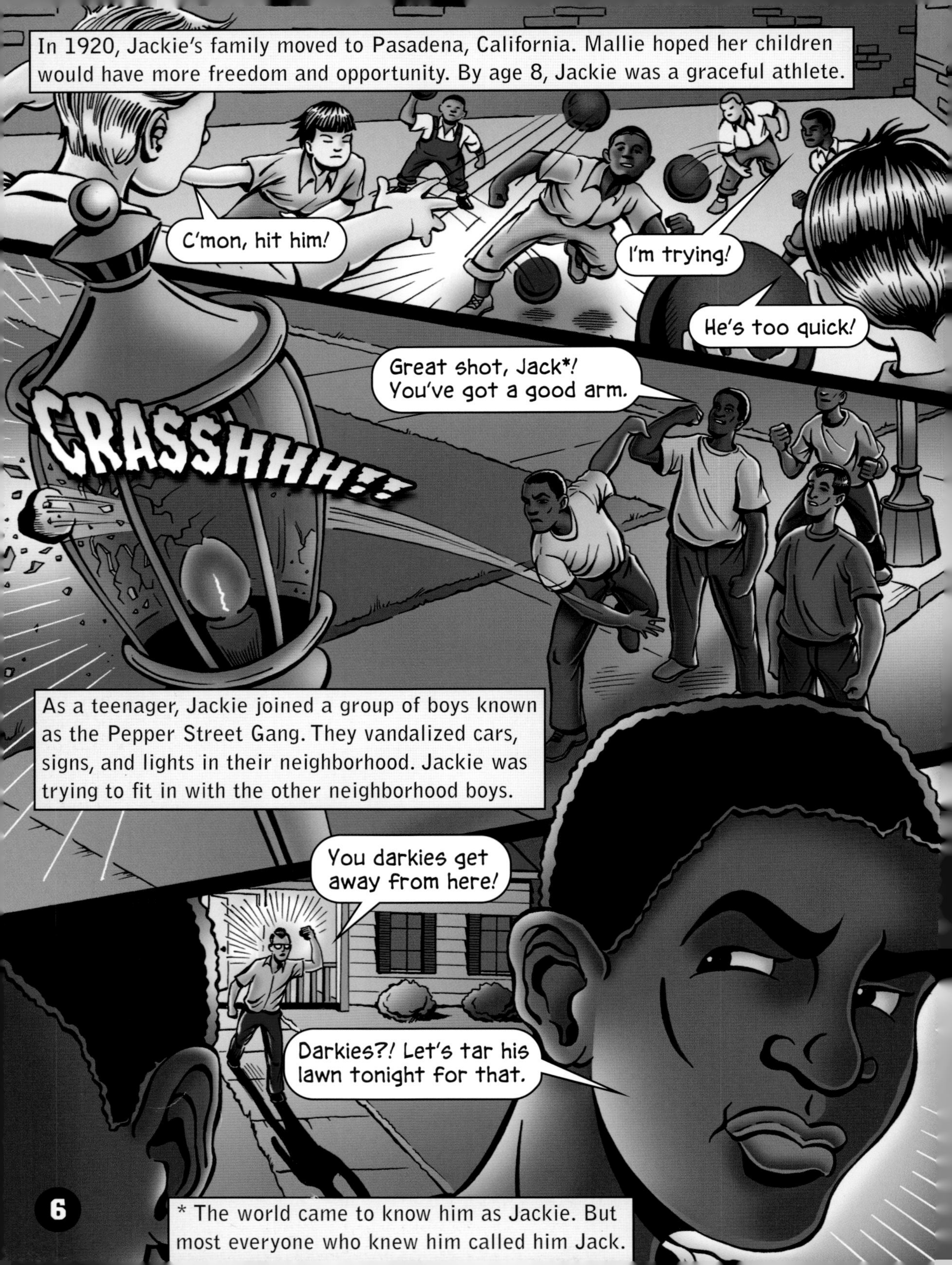
In 1920, Jackie's family moved to Pasadena, California. Mallie hoped her children would have more freedom and opportunity. By age 8, Jackie was a graceful athlete.
C'mon, hit him!
I'm trying!
He's too quick!
CRASSHHHH!!
Great shot, Jack*! You've got a good arm.
As a teenager, Jackie joined a group of boys known as the Pepper Street Gang. They vandalized cars, signs, and lights in their neighborhood. Jackie was trying to fit in with the other neighborhood boys.
You darkies get away from here!
Darkies?! Let's tar his lawn tonight for that.
* The world came to know him as Jackie. But most everyone who knew him called him Jack.

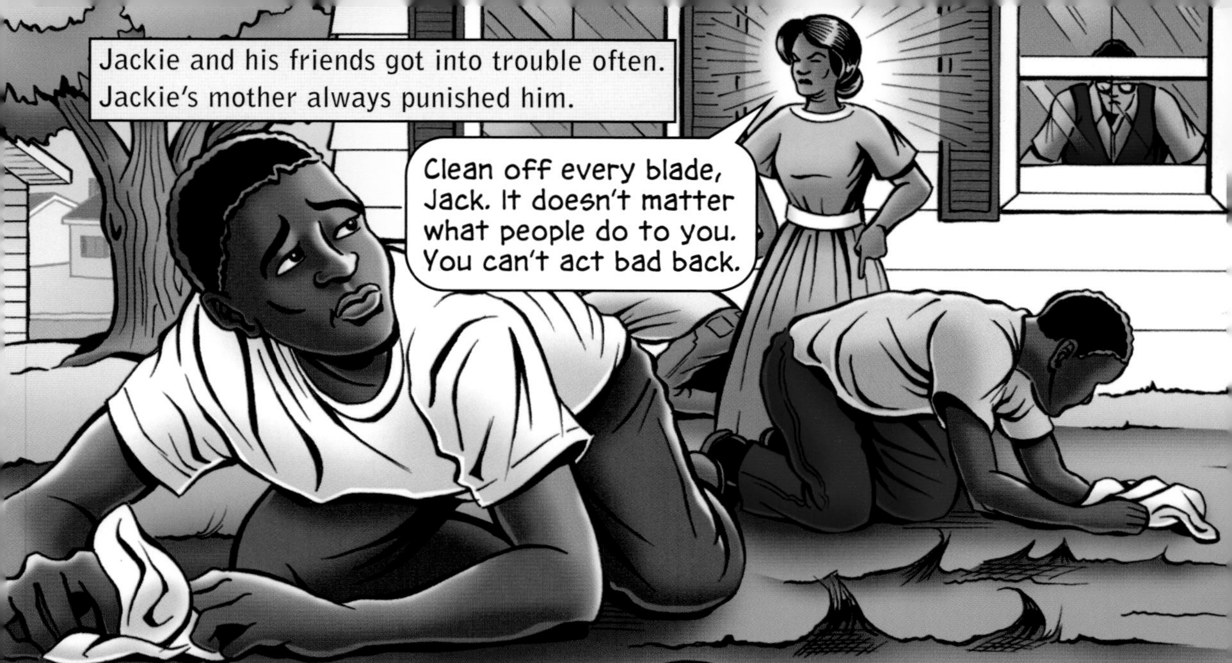
Jackie and his friends got into trouble often. Jackie's mother always punished him.
Clean off every blade, Jack. It doesn't matter what people do to you. You can't act bad back.

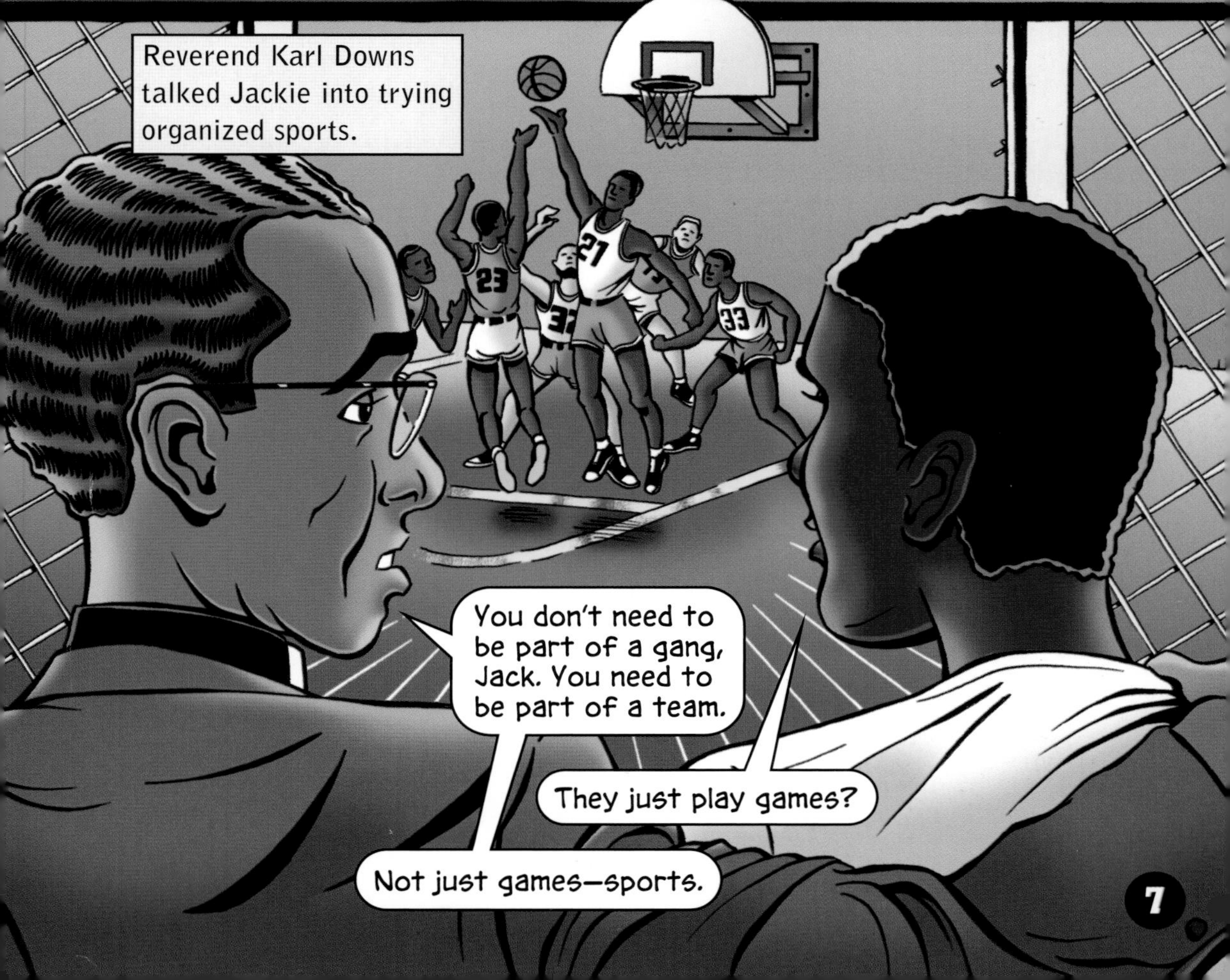
Reverend Karl Downs talked Jackie into trying organized sports.
You don't need to be part of a gang, Jack. You need to be part of a team.
They just play games?
Not just games—sports.

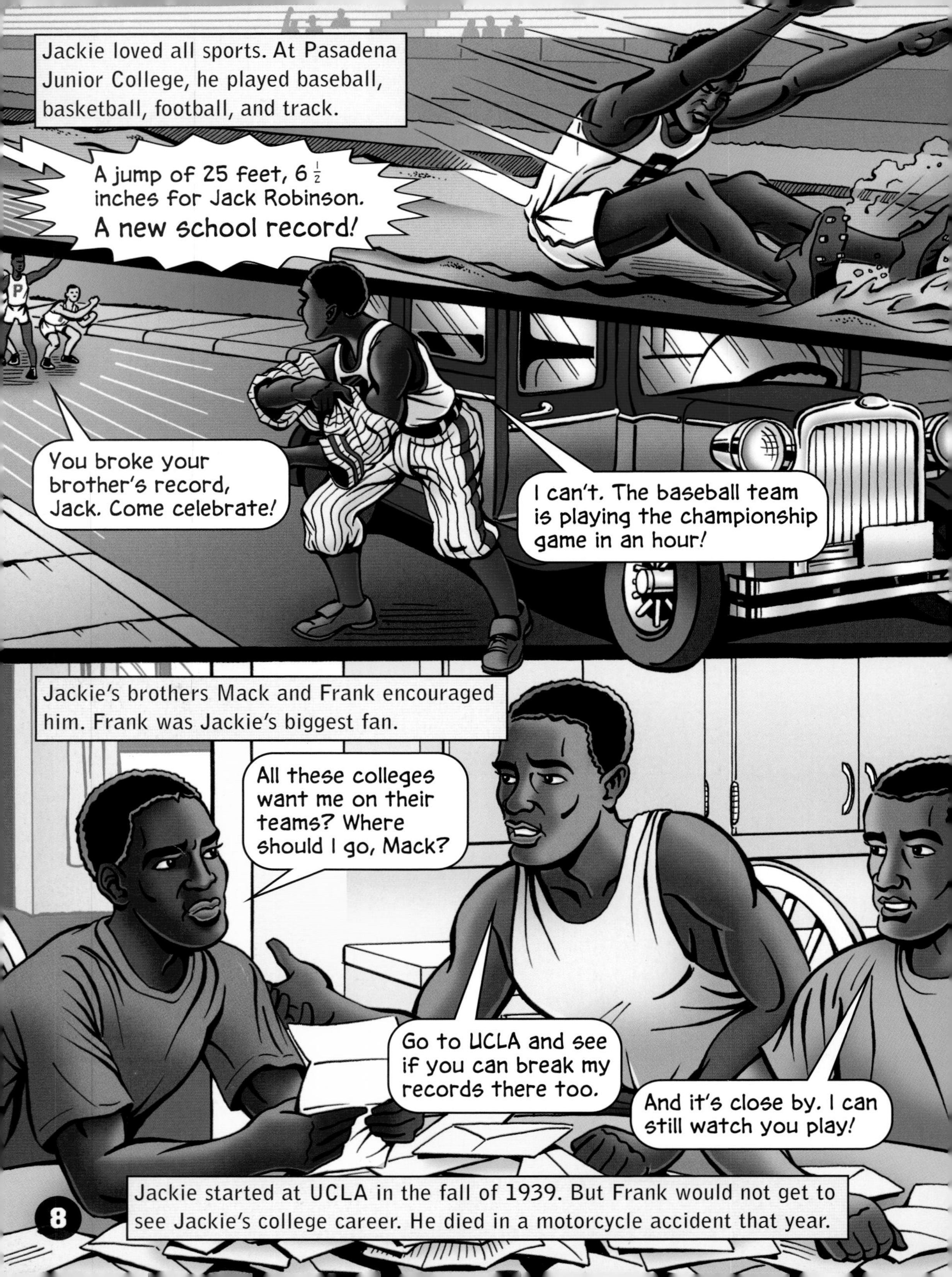
Jackie loved all sports. At Pasadena Junior College, he played baseball, basketball, football, and track.
A jump of 25 feet, 6 $\frac{1}{2}$ inches for Jack Robinson. A new school record!
You broke your brother's record, Jack. Come celebrate!
I can't. The baseball team is playing the championship game in an hour!
Jackie's brothers Mack and Frank encouraged him. Frank was Jackie's biggest fan.
All these colleges want me on their teams? Where should I go, Mack?
Go to UCLA and see if you can break my records there too.
And it's close by. I can still watch you play!
Jackie started at UCLA in the fall of 1939. But Frank would not get to see Jackie's college career. He died in a motorcycle accident that year.

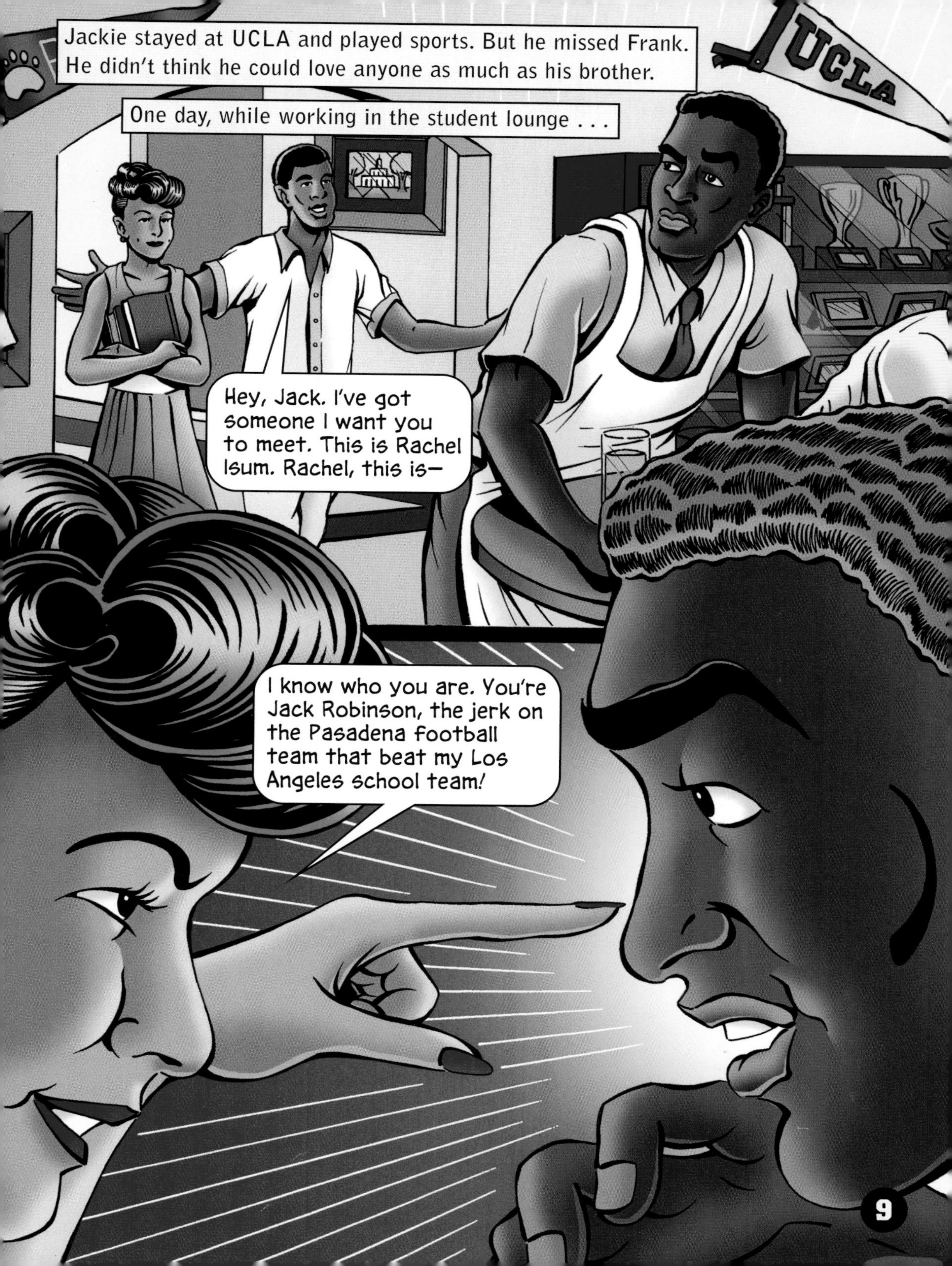
Jackie stayed at UCLA and played sports. But he missed Frank. He didn't think he could love anyone as much as his brother.
UCLA
One day, while working in the student lounge . . .
Hey, Jack. I've got someone I want you to meet. This is Rachel Isum. Rachel, this is—
I know who you are. You're Jack Robinson, the jerk on the Pasadena football team that beat my Los Angeles school team!

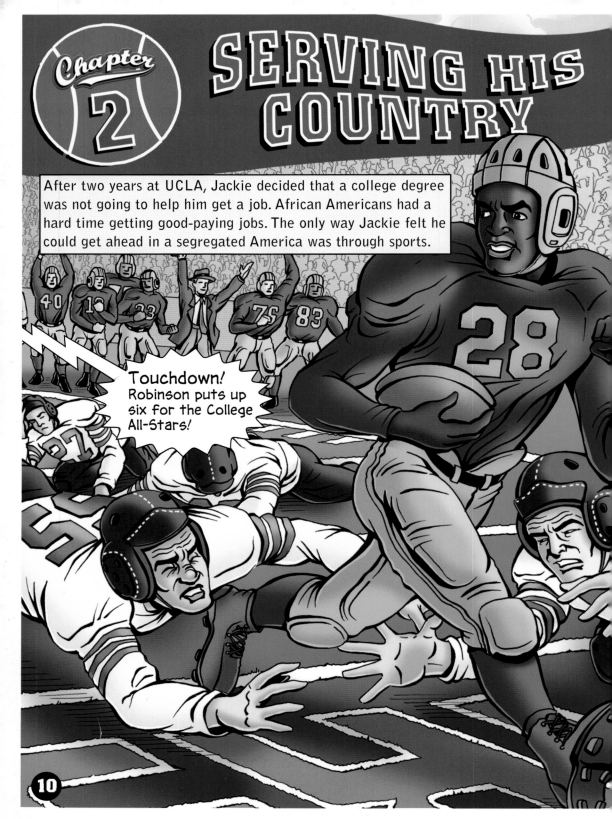

Chapter 2

SERVING HIS COUNTRY

After two years at UCLA, Jackie decided that a college degree was not going to help him get a job. African Americans had a hard time getting good-paying jobs. The only way Jackie felt he could get ahead in a segregated America was through sports.

Touchdown! Robinson puts up six for the College All-Stars!

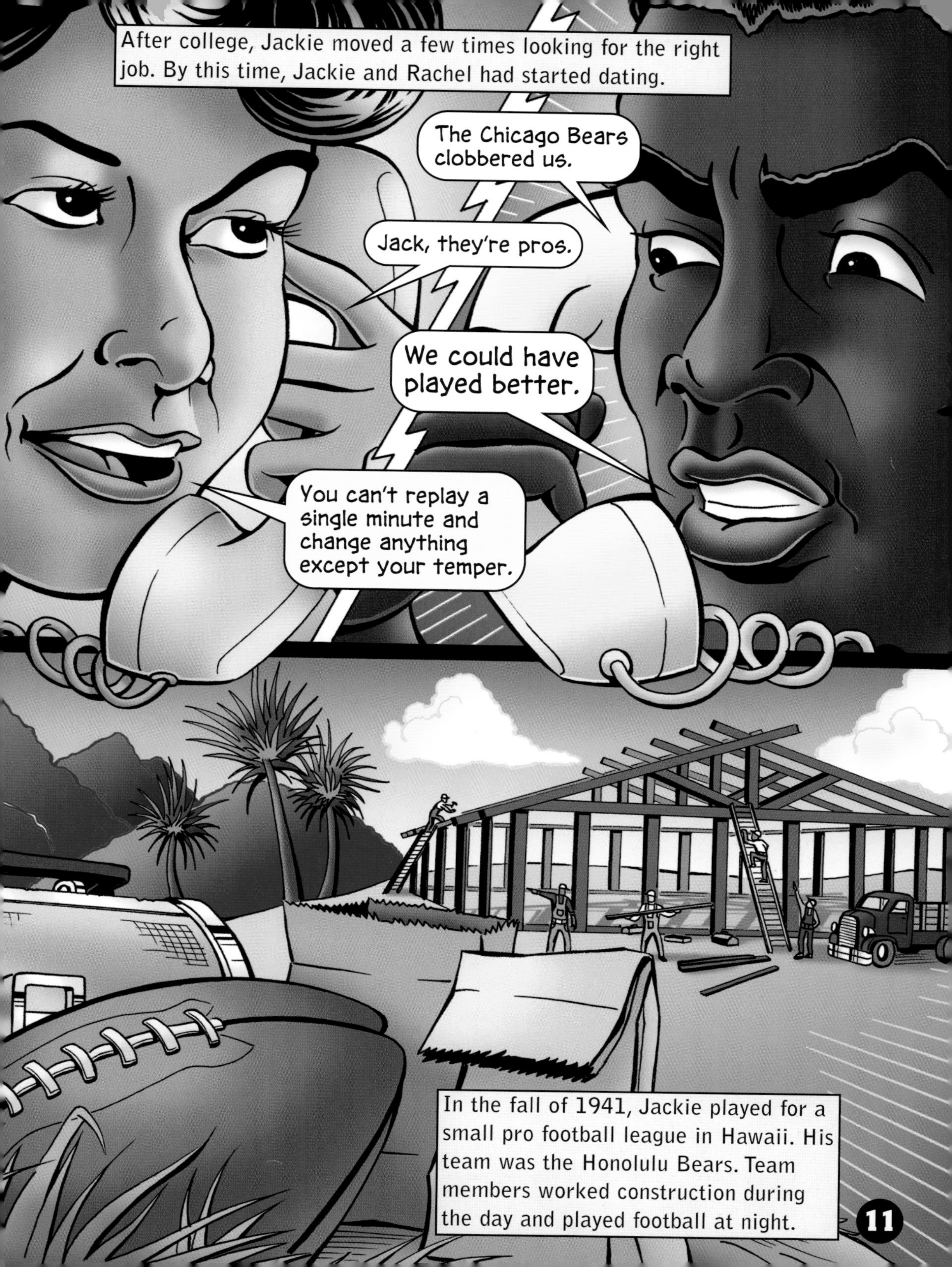
After college, Jackie moved a few times looking for the right job. By this time, Jackie and Rachel had started dating.
The Chicago Bears clobbered us.
Jack, they're pros.
We could have played better.
You can't replay a single minute and change anything except your temper.
In the fall of 1941, Jackie played for a small pro football league in Hawaii. His team was the Honolulu Bears. Team members worked construction during the day and played football at night.

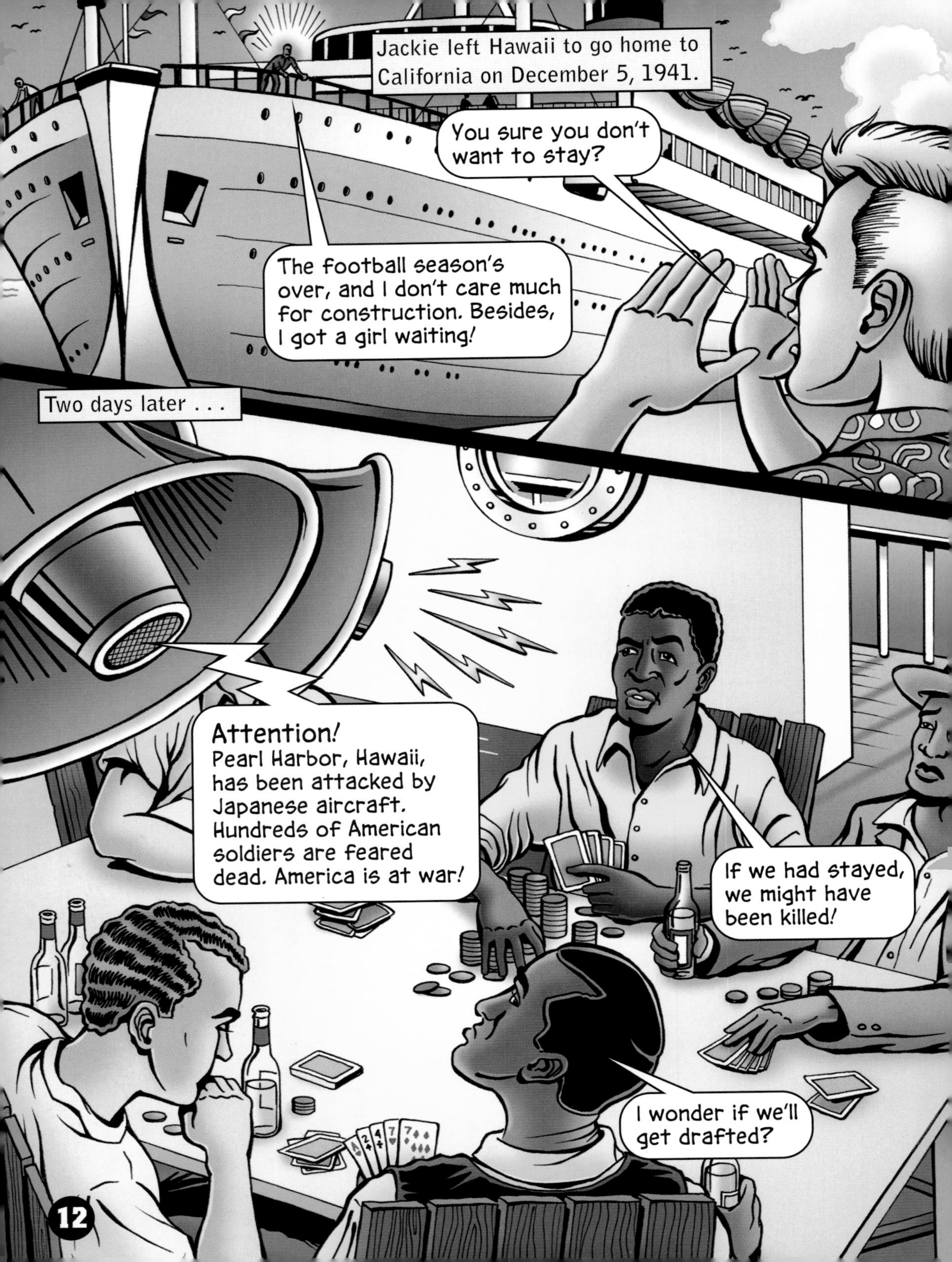

Jackie left Hawaii to go home to California on December 5, 1941.
You sure you don't want to stay?
The football season's over, and I don't care much for construction. Besides, I got a girl waiting!
Two days later . . .
Attention! Pearl Harbor, Hawaii, has been attacked by Japanese aircraft. Hundreds of American soldiers are feared dead. America is at war!
If we had stayed, we might have been killed!
I wonder if we'll get drafted?

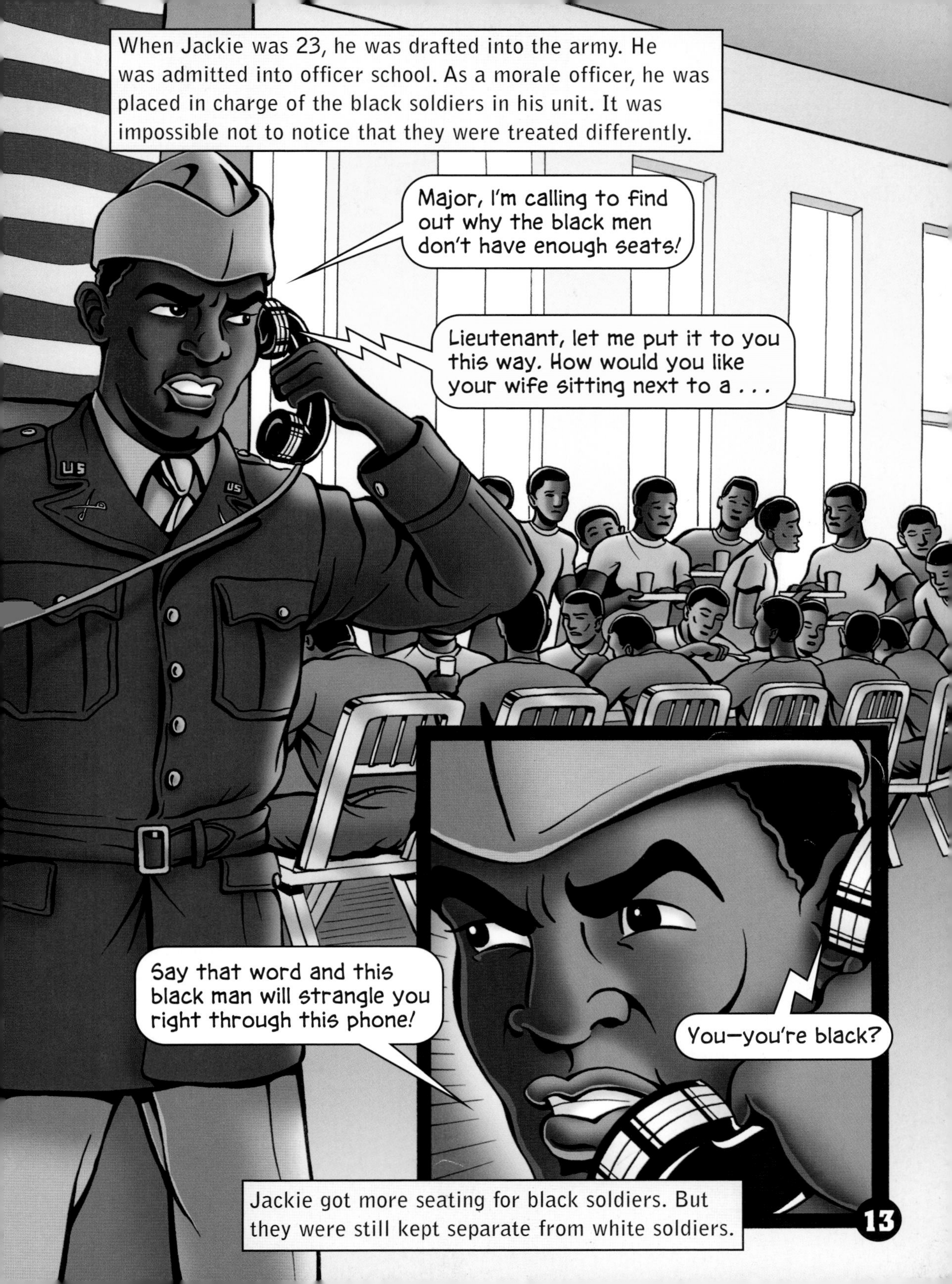
When Jackie was 23, he was drafted into the army. He was admitted into officer school. As a morale officer, he was placed in charge of the black soldiers in his unit. It was impossible not to notice that they were treated differently.
Major, I'm calling to find out why the black men don't have enough seats!
Lieutenant, let me put it to you this way. How would you like your wife sitting next to a . . .
Say that word and this black man will strangle you right through this phone!
You—you're black?
Jackie got more seating for black soldiers. But they were still kept separate from white soldiers.

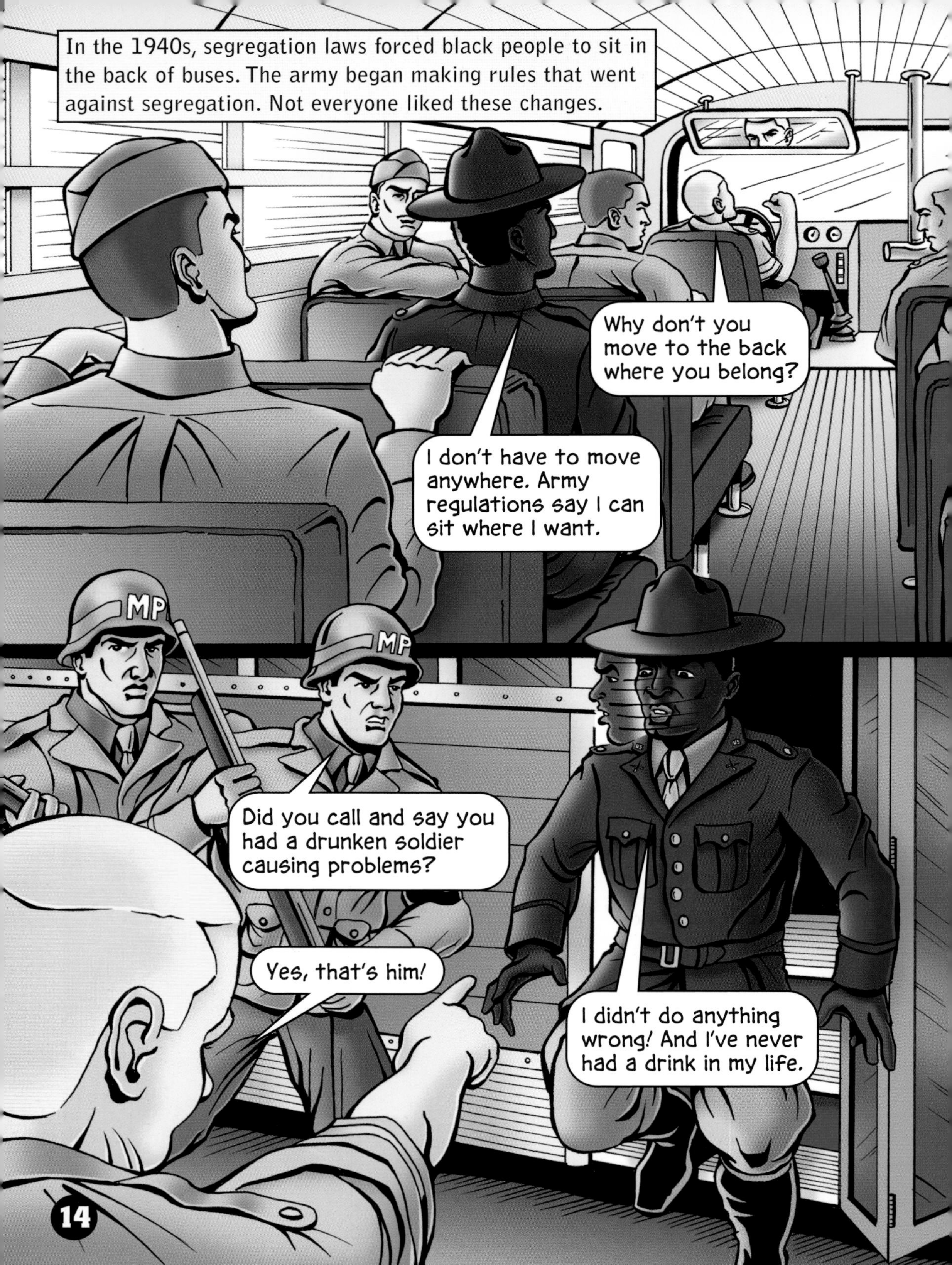
In the 1940s, segregation laws forced black people to sit in the back of buses. The army began making rules that went against segregation. Not everyone liked these changes.
Why don't you move to the back where you belong?
I don't have to move anywhere. Army regulations say I can sit where I want.
MP
MP
Did you call and say you had a drunken soldier causing problems?
Yes, that's him!
I didn't do anything wrong! And I've never had a drink in my life.

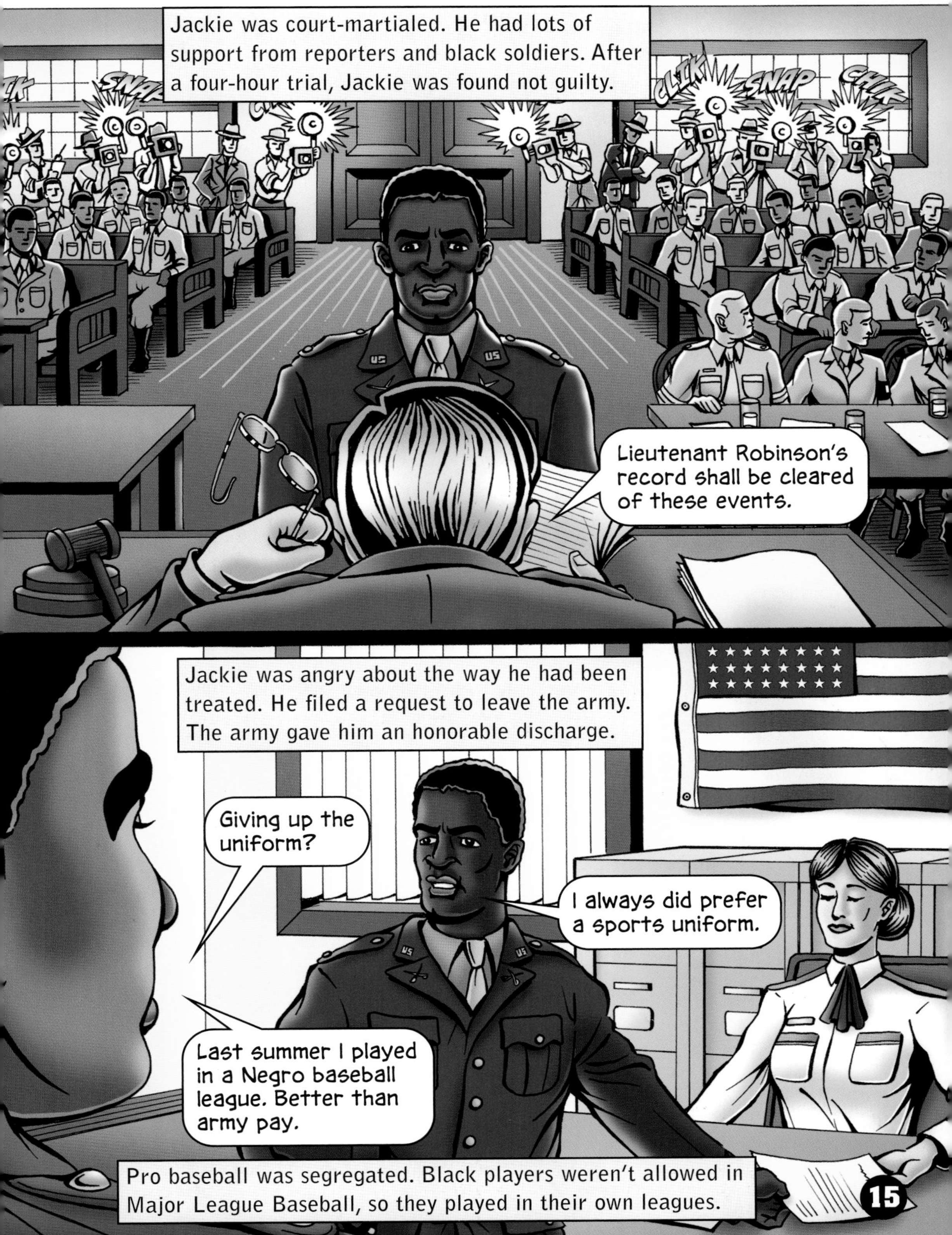
Jackie was court-martialed. He had lots of support from reporters and black soldiers. After a four-hour trial, Jackie was found not guilty.
SNAP
CLIK
SNAP
CHIK
Lieutenant Robinson's record shall be cleared of these events.
Jackie was angry about the way he had been treated. He filed a request to leave the army. The army gave him an honorable discharge.
Giving up the uniform?
I always did prefer a sports uniform.
Last summer I played in a Negro baseball league. Better than army pay.
Pro baseball was segregated. Black players weren't allowed in Major League Baseball, so they played in their own leagues.

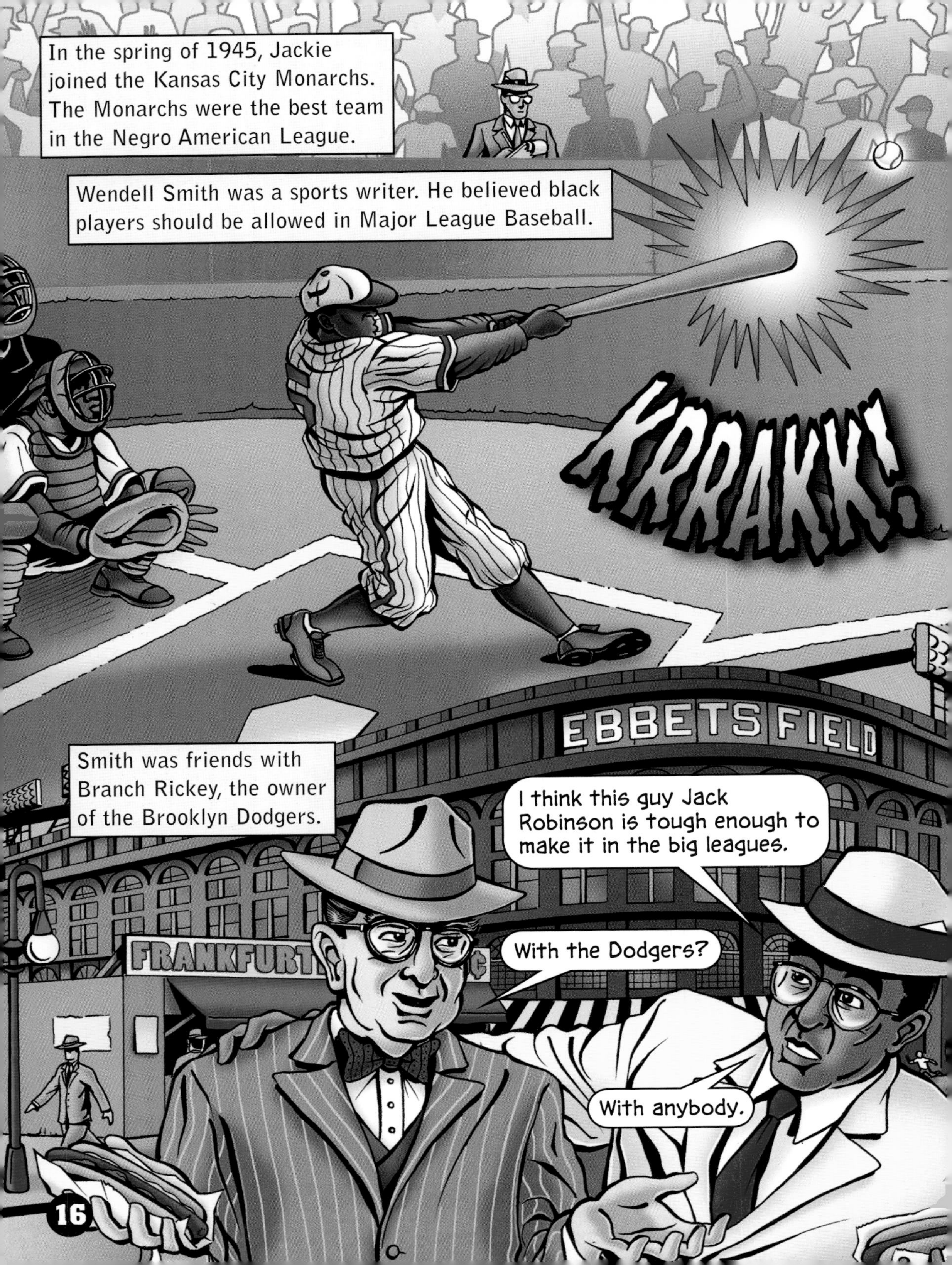
In the spring of 1945, Jackie joined the Kansas City Monarchs. The Monarchs were the best team in the Negro American League.
Wendell Smith was a sports writer. He believed black players should be allowed in Major League Baseball.
KRRAKK!
EBBETS FIELD
Smith was friends with Branch Rickey, the owner of the Brooklyn Dodgers.
I think this guy Jack Robinson is tough enough to make it in the big leagues.
With the Dodgers?
With anybody.

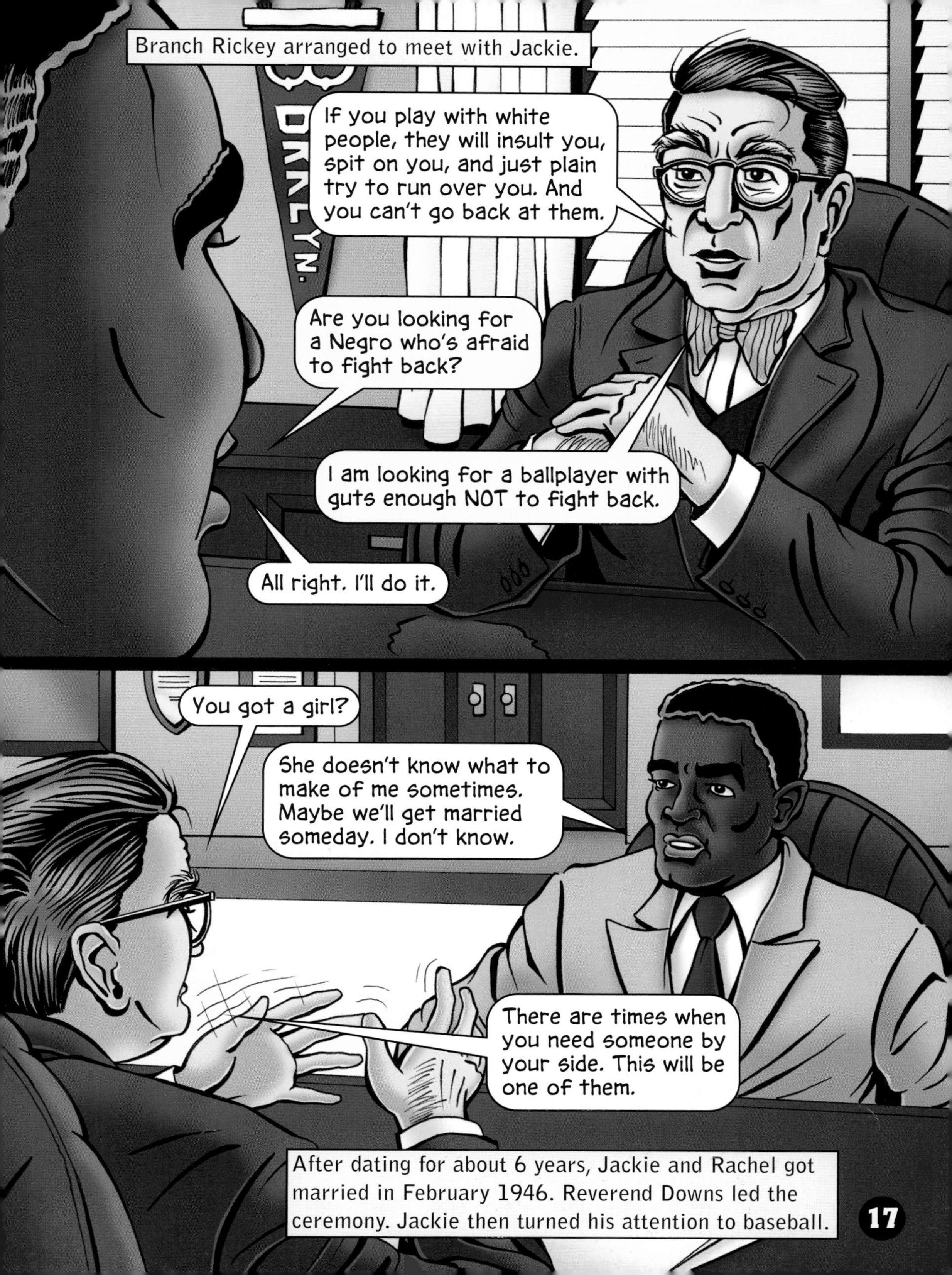
Branch Rickey arranged to meet with Jackie.
If you play with white people, they will insult you, spit on you, and just plain try to run over you. And you can't go back at them.
Are you looking for a Negro who's afraid to fight back?
I am looking for a ballplayer with guts enough NOT to fight back.
All right. I'll do it.
You got a girl?
She doesn't know what to make of me sometimes. Maybe we'll get married someday. I don't know.
There are times when you need someone by your side. This will be one of them.
After dating for about 6 years, Jackie and Rachel got married in February 1946. Reverend Downs led the ceremony. Jackie then turned his attention to baseball.

Chapter 3
INTEGRATING BASEBALL

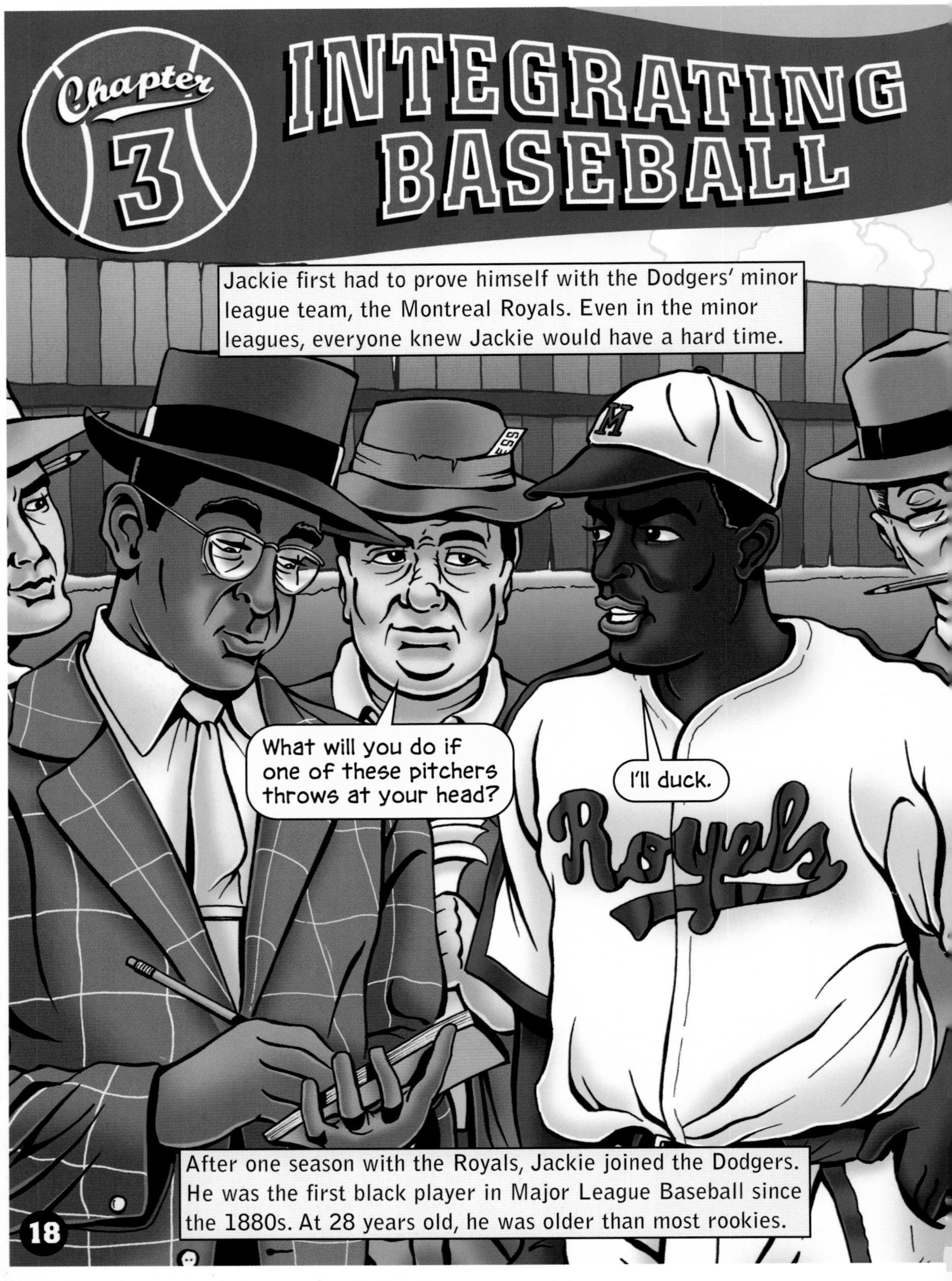
Jackie first had to prove himself with the Dodgers' minor league team, the Montreal Royals. Even in the minor leagues, everyone knew Jackie would have a hard time.
What will you do if one of these pitchers throws at your head?
I'll duck.
Royals
After one season with the Royals, Jackie joined the Dodgers. He was the first black player in Major League Baseball since the 1880s. At 28 years old, he was older than most rookies.

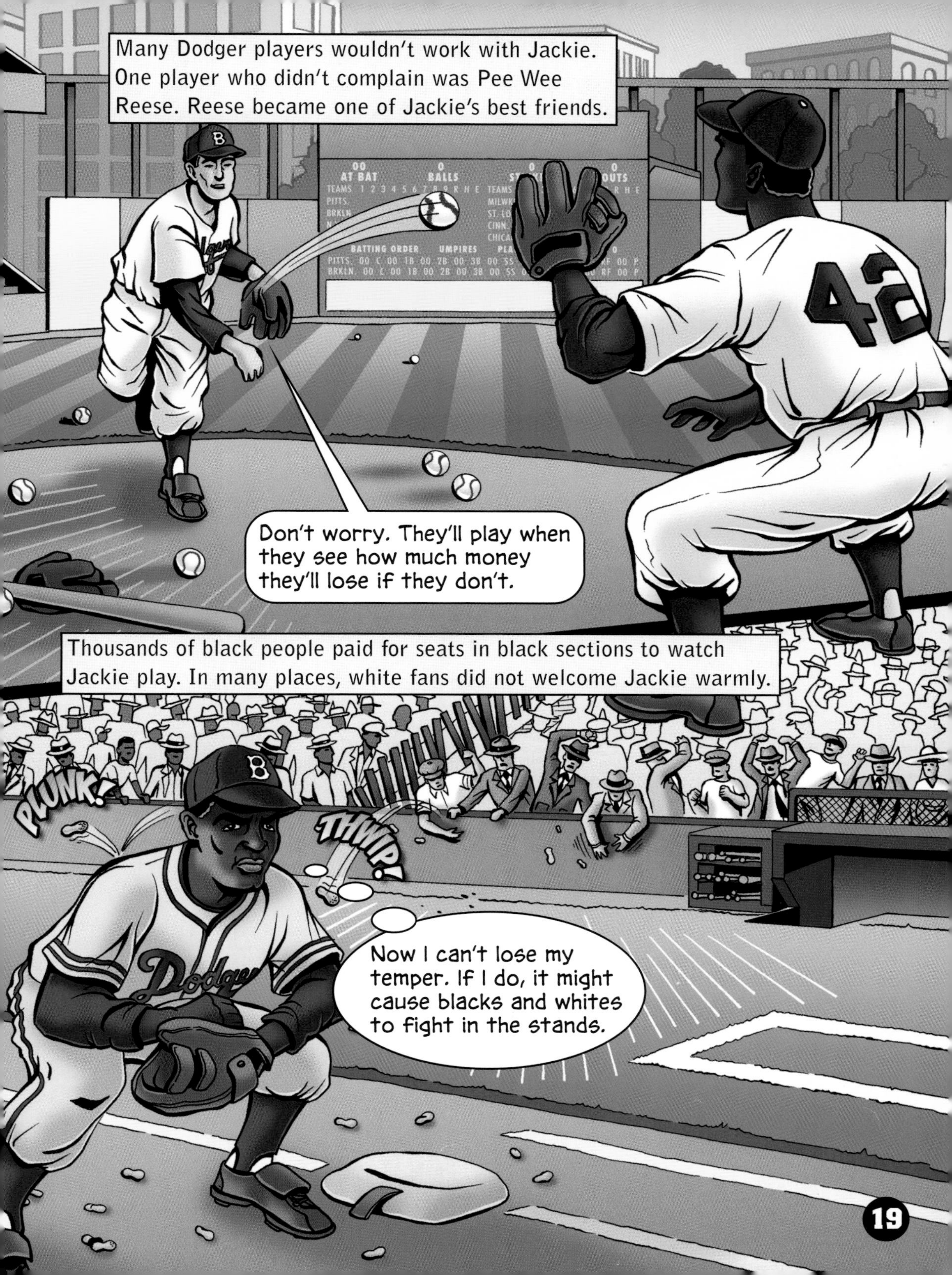

Many Dodger players wouldn't work with Jackie. One player who didn't complain was Pee Wee Reese. Reese became one of Jackie's best friends.
Don't worry. They'll play when they see how much money they'll lose if they don't.
Thousands of black people paid for seats in black sections to watch Jackie play. In many places, white fans did not welcome Jackie warmly.
PLUNK!
THWIP!
Now I can't lose my temper. If I do, it might cause blacks and whites to fight in the stands.

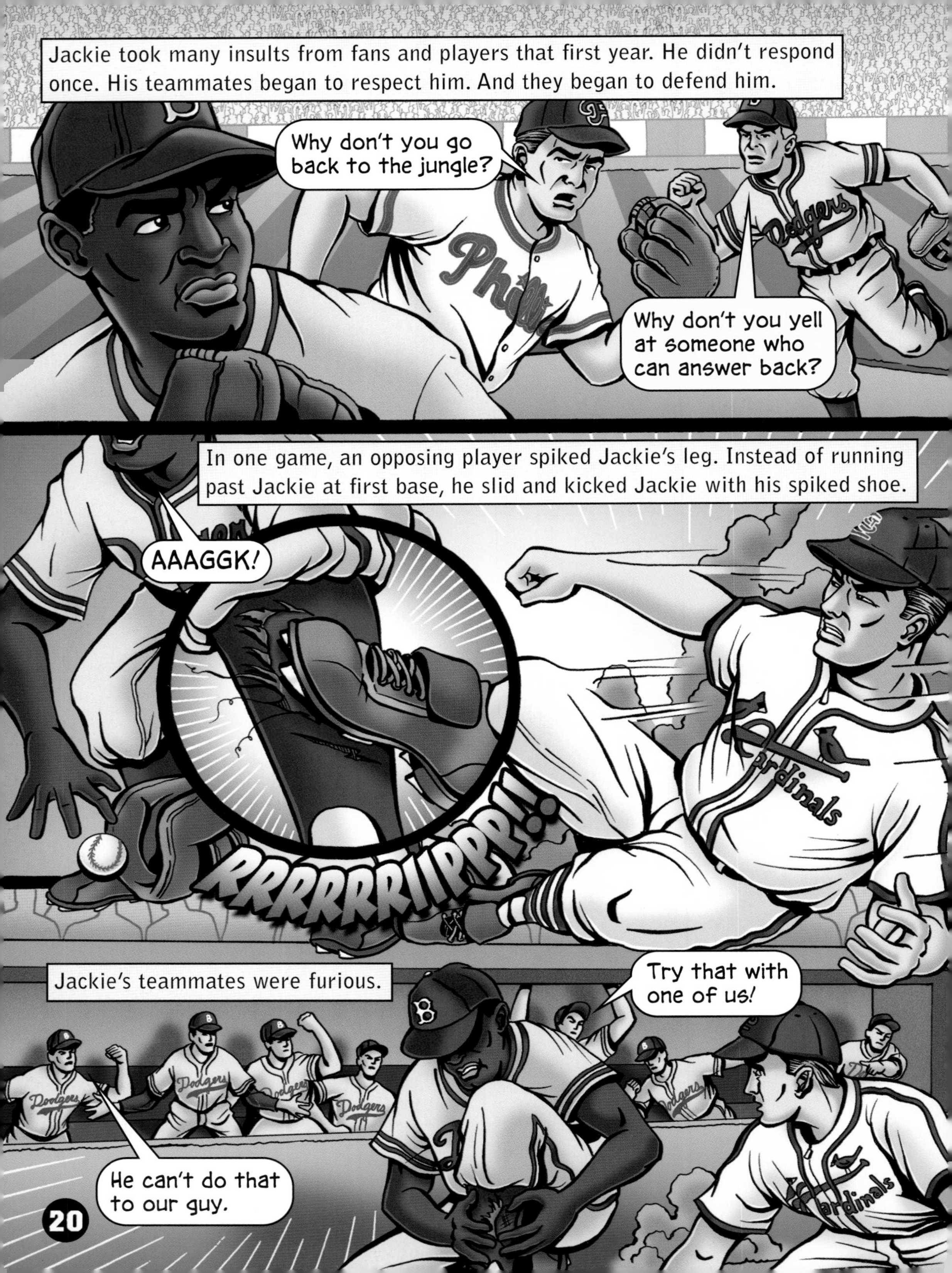
Jackie took many insults from fans and players that first year. He didn't respond once. His teammates began to respect him. And they began to defend him.
Why don't you go back to the jungle?
Why don't you yell at someone who can answer back?
In one game, an opposing player spiked Jackie's leg. Instead of running past Jackie at first base, he slid and kicked Jackie with his spiked shoe.
AAAGGK!
RRRRRRRIIPPP!!
Jackie's teammates were furious.
Try that with one of us!
He can't do that to our guy.

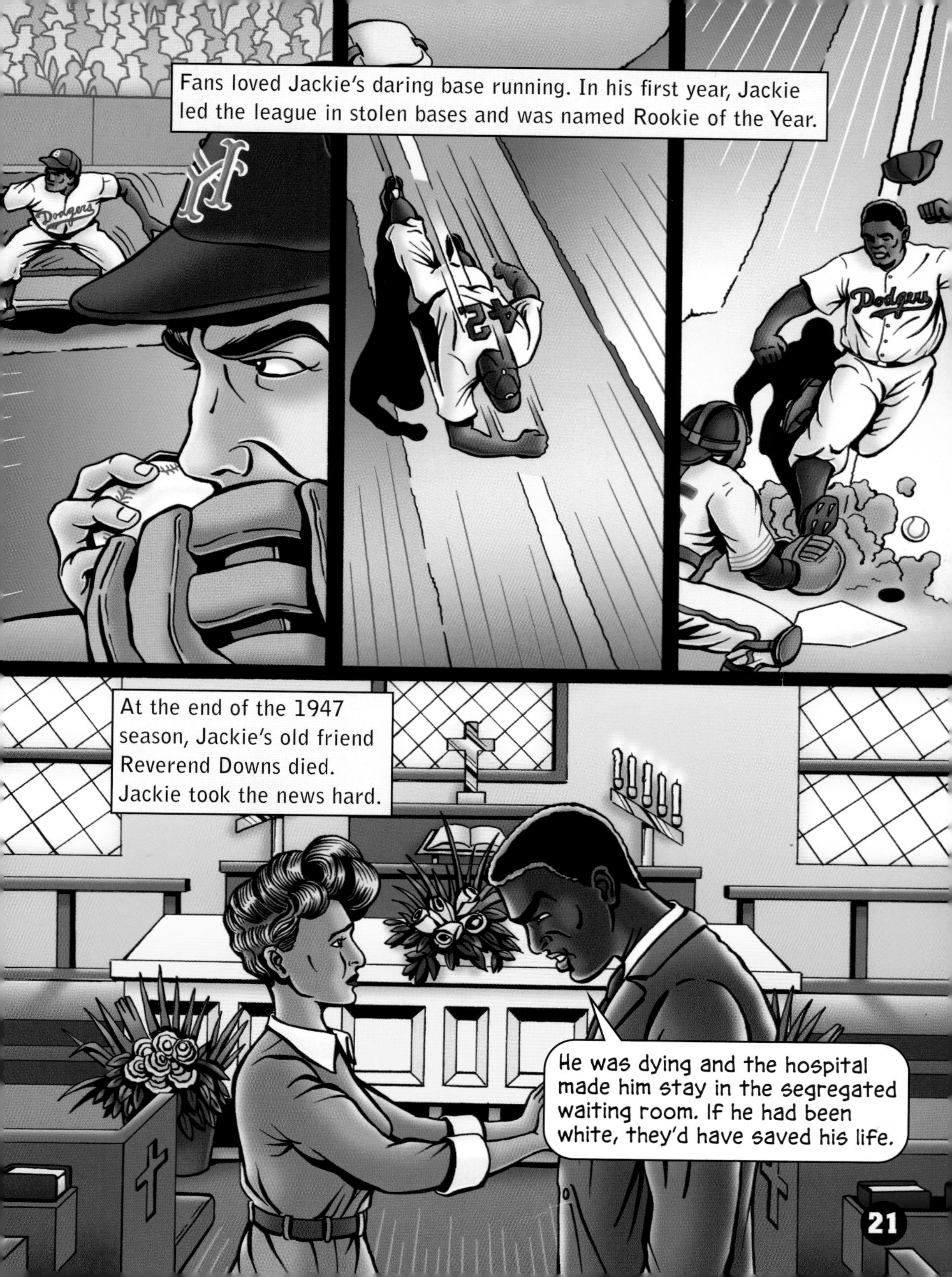
Fans loved Jackie's daring base running. In his first year, Jackie led the league in stolen bases and was named Rookie of the Year.
42
At the end of the 1947 season, Jackie's old friend Reverend Downs died. Jackie took the news hard.
He was dying and the hospital made him stay in the segregated waiting room. If he had been white, they'd have saved his life.

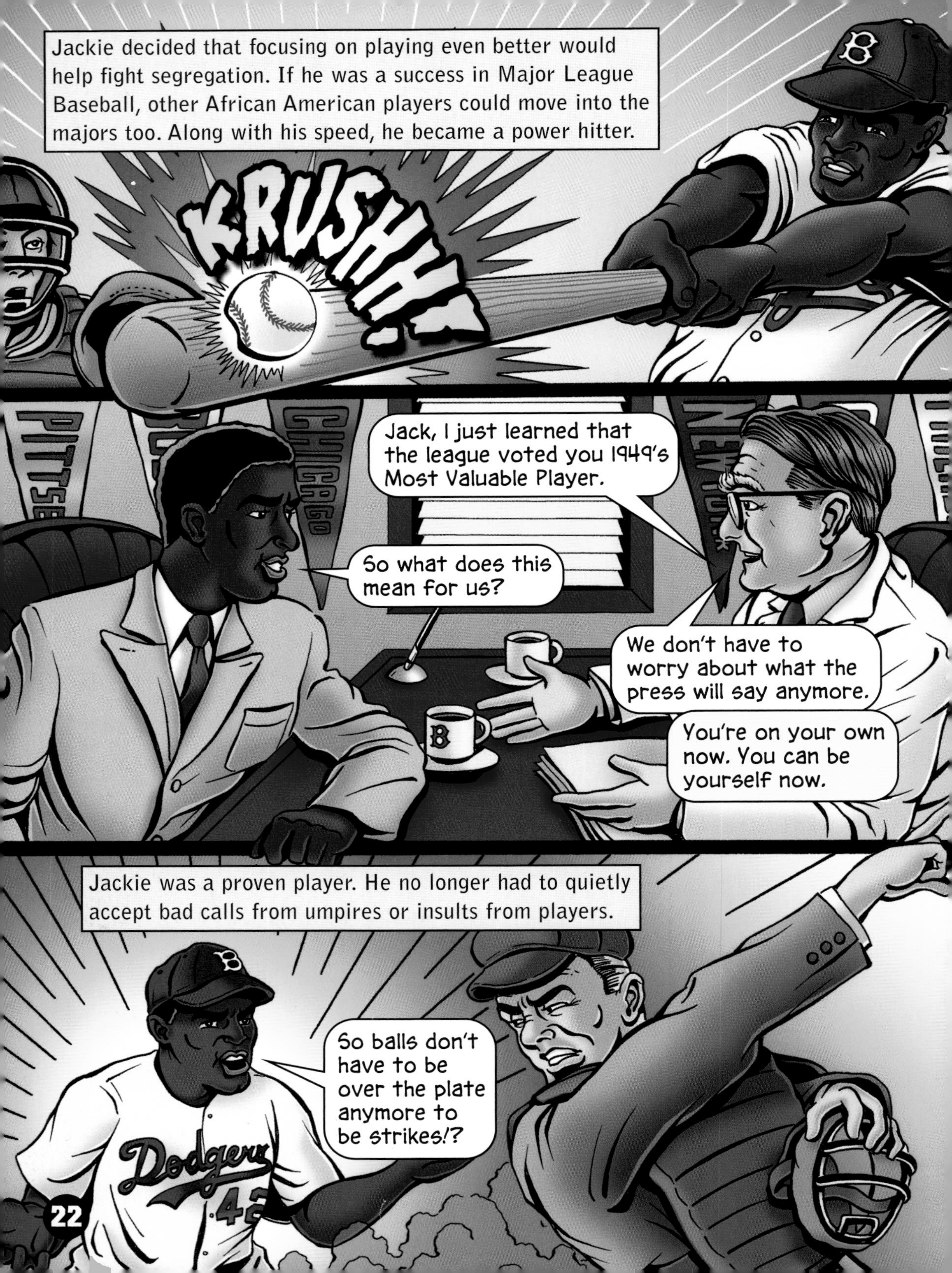
Jackie decided that focusing on playing even better would help fight segregation. If he was a success in Major League Baseball, other African American players could move into the majors too. Along with his speed, he became a power hitter.
KRUSH!
Jack, I just learned that the league voted you 1949's Most Valuable Player.
So what does this mean for us?
We don't have to worry about what the press will say anymore.
You're on your own now. You can be yourself now.
Jackie was a proven player. He no longer had to quietly accept bad calls from umpires or insults from players.
So balls don't have to be over the plate anymore to be strikes!?

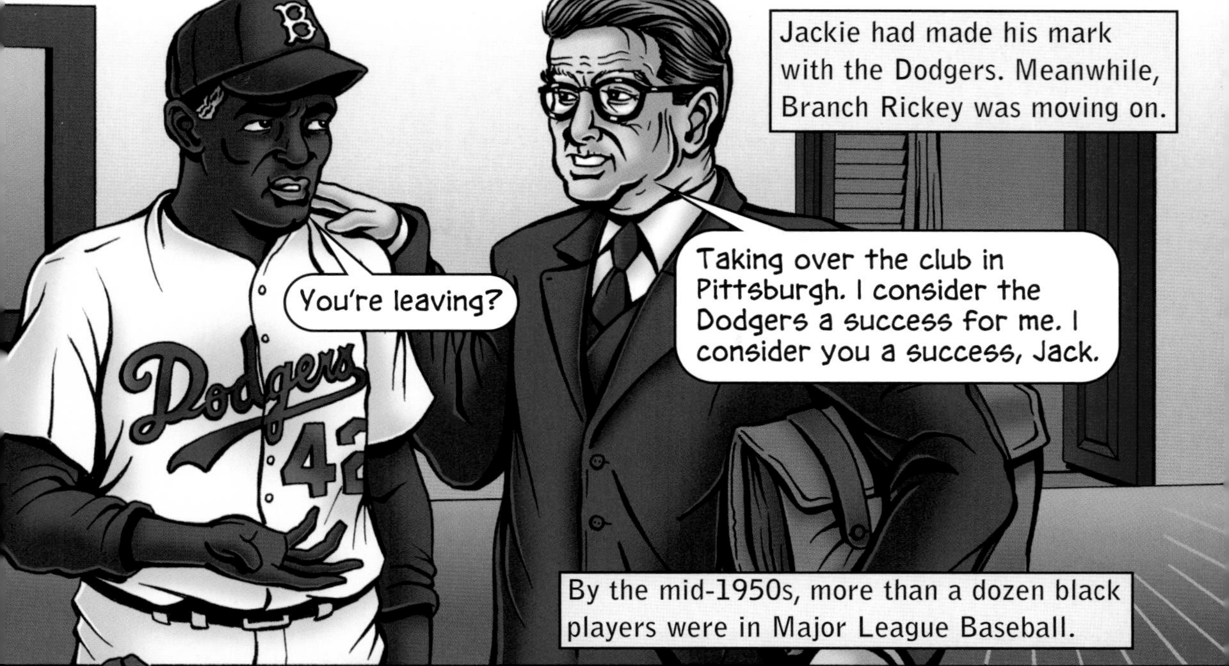
Jackie had made his mark with the Dodgers. Meanwhile, Branch Rickey was moving on.
You're leaving?
Taking over the club in Pittsburgh. I consider the Dodgers a success for me. I consider you a success, Jack.
By the mid-1950s, more than a dozen black players were in Major League Baseball.

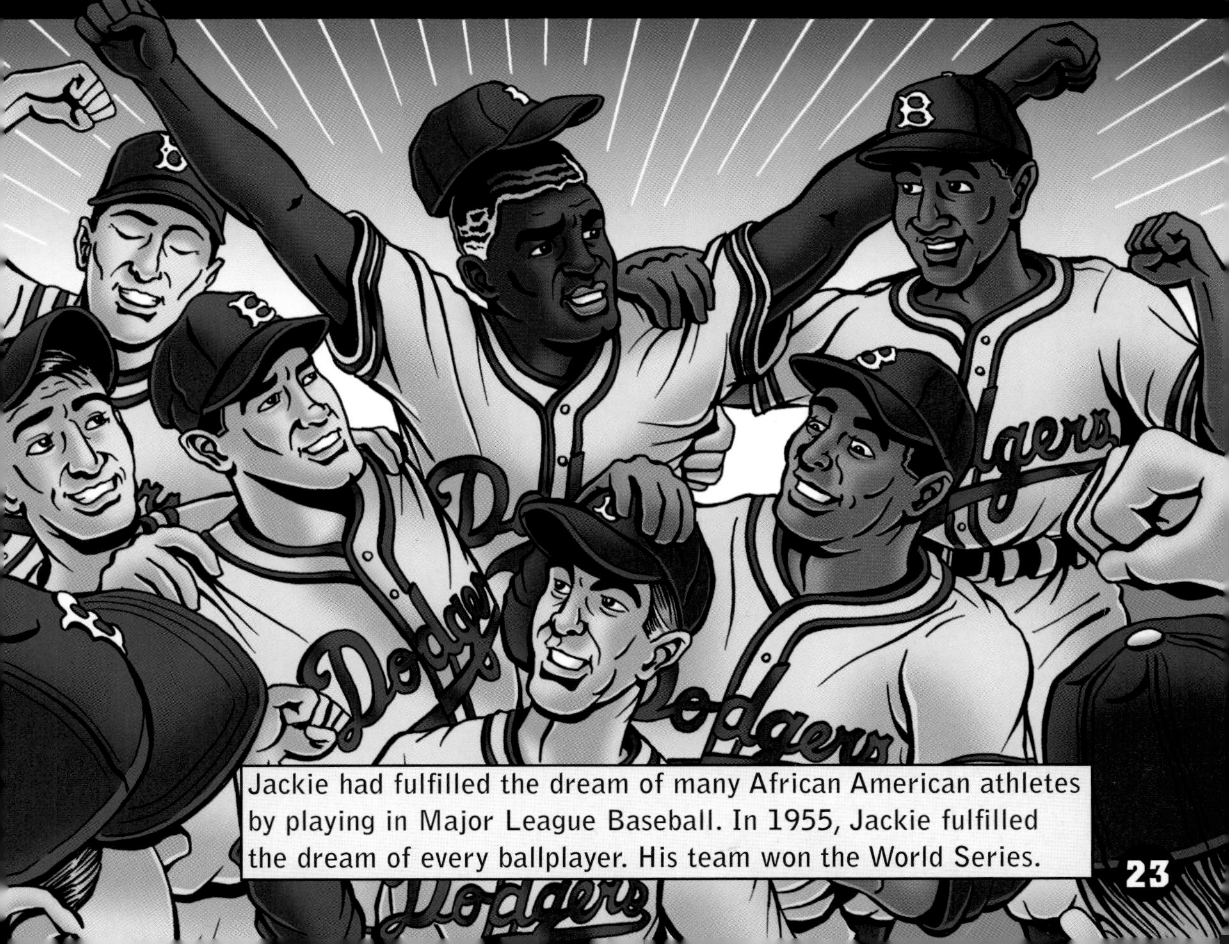
Jackie had fulfilled the dream of many African American athletes by playing in Major League Baseball. In 1955, Jackie fulfilled the dream of every ballplayer. His team won the World Series.

Chapter 4 NEVER HAD IT MADE

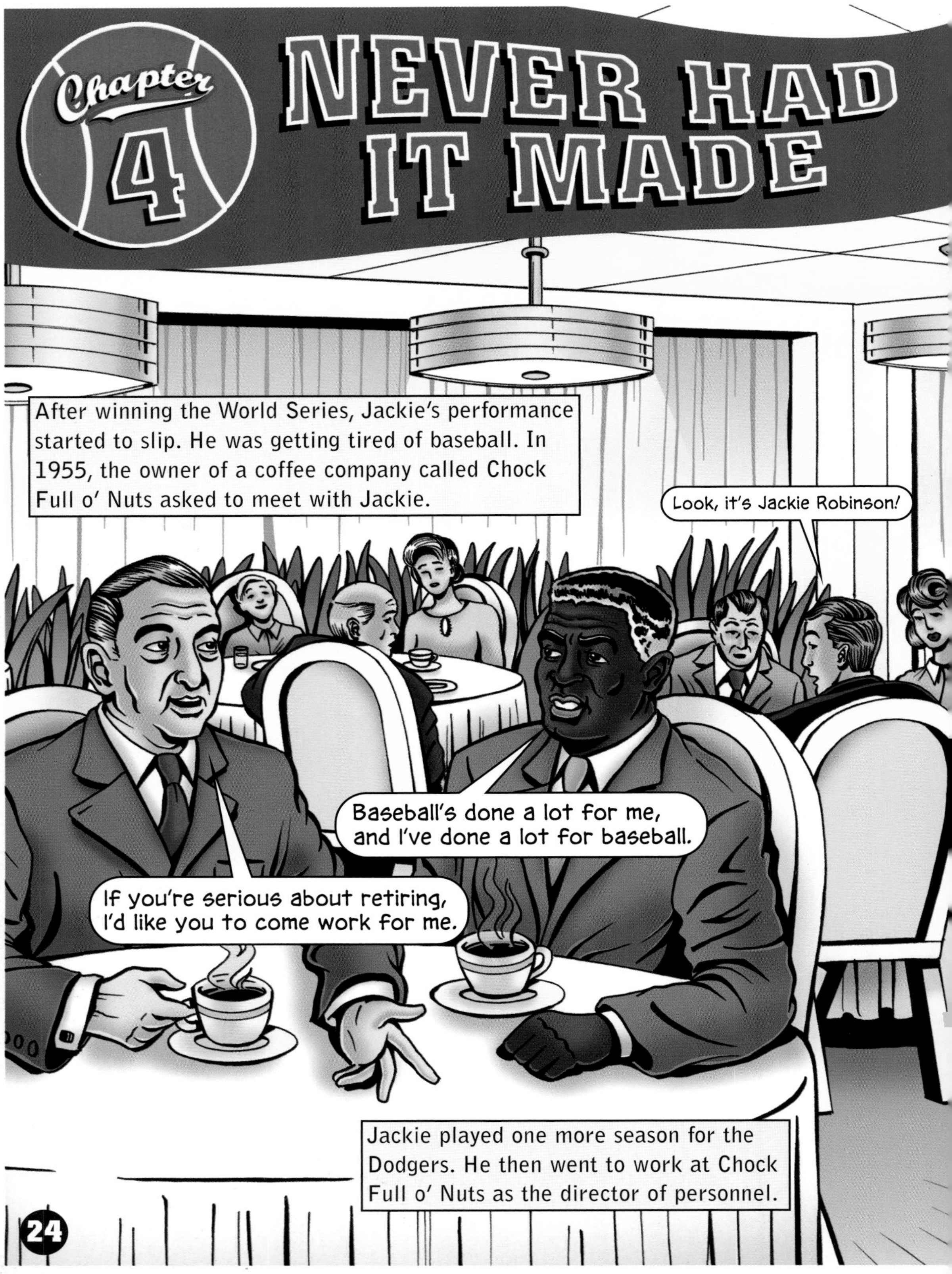
After winning the World Series, Jackie's performance started to slip. He was getting tired of baseball. In 1955, the owner of a coffee company called Chock Full o' Nuts asked to meet with Jackie.
Look, it's Jackie Robinson!
Baseball's done a lot for me, and I've done a lot for baseball.
If you're serious about retiring, I'd like you to come work for me.
Jackie played one more season for the Dodgers. He then went to work at Chock Full o' Nuts as the director of personnel.

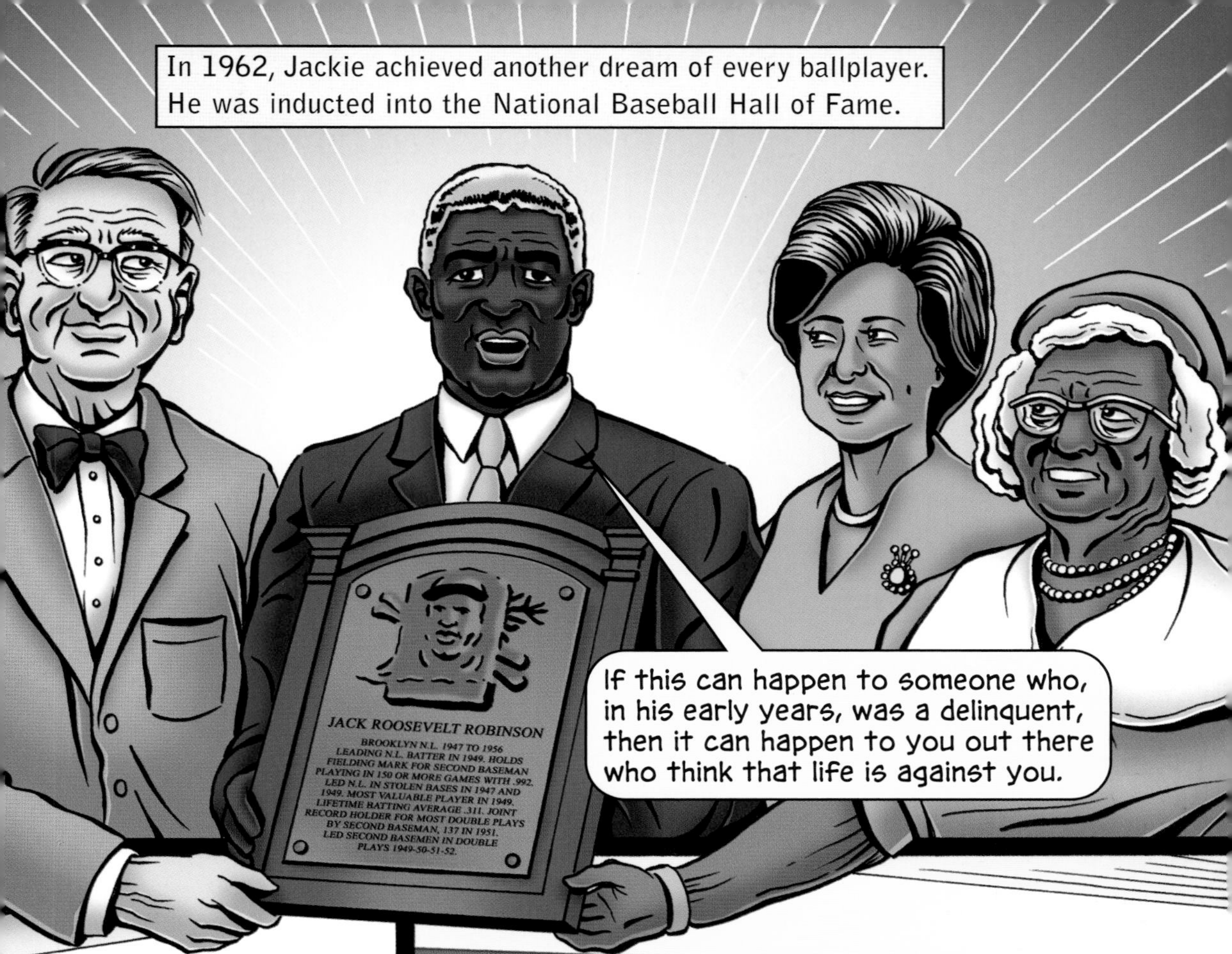
In 1962, Jackie achieved another dream of every ballplayer. He was inducted into the National Baseball Hall of Fame.
JACK ROOSEVELT ROBINSON
BROOKLYN N.L. 1947 TO 1956 LEADING N.L. BATTER IN 1949. HOLDS FIELDING MARK FOR SECOND BASEMAN PLAYING IN 150 OR MORE GAMES WITH .992. LED N.L. IN STOLEN BASES IN 1947 AND 1949. MOST VALUABLE PLAYER IN 1949. LIFETIME BATTING AVERAGE .311. JOINT RECORD HOLDER FOR MOST DOUBLE PLAYS BY SECOND BASEMAN, 137 IN 1951. LED SECOND BASEMEN IN DOUBLE PLAYS 1949-50-51-52.
If this can happen to someone who, in his early years, was a delinquent, then it can happen to you out there who think that life is against you.

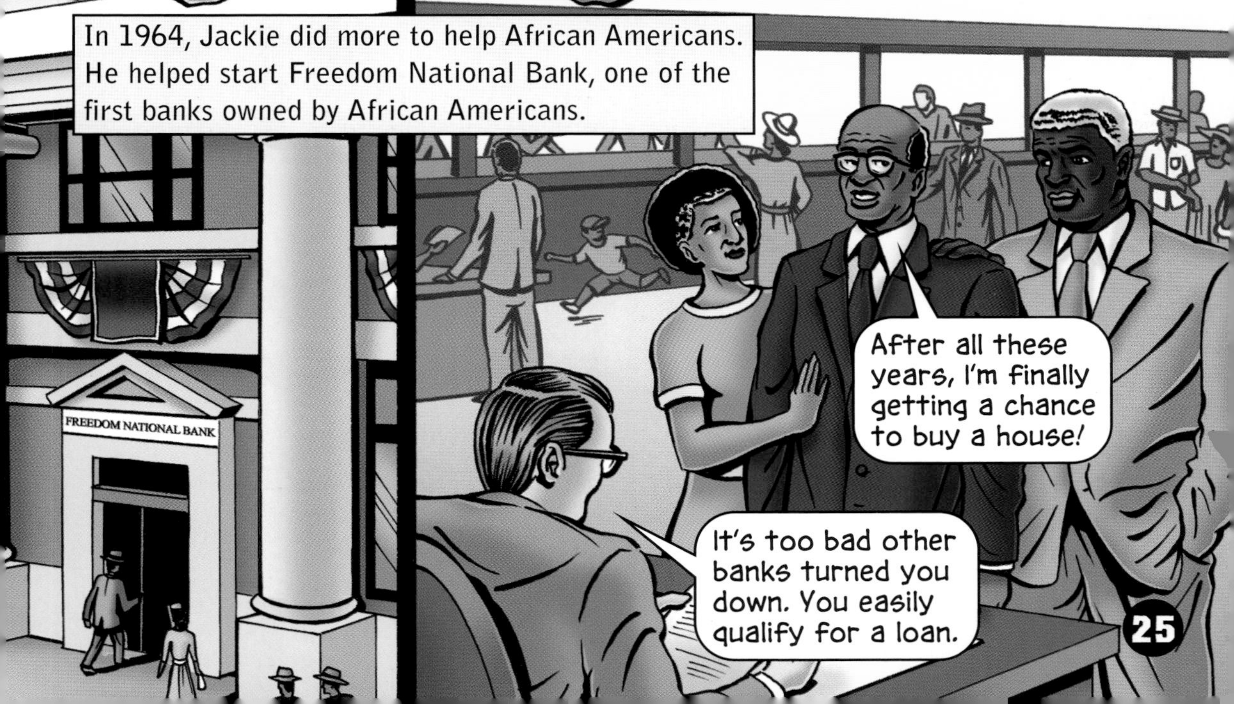
In 1964, Jackie did more to help African Americans. He helped start Freedom National Bank, one of the first banks owned by African Americans.
FREEDOM NATIONAL BANK
After all these years, I'm finally getting a chance to buy a house!
It's too bad other banks turned you down. You easily qualify for a loan.

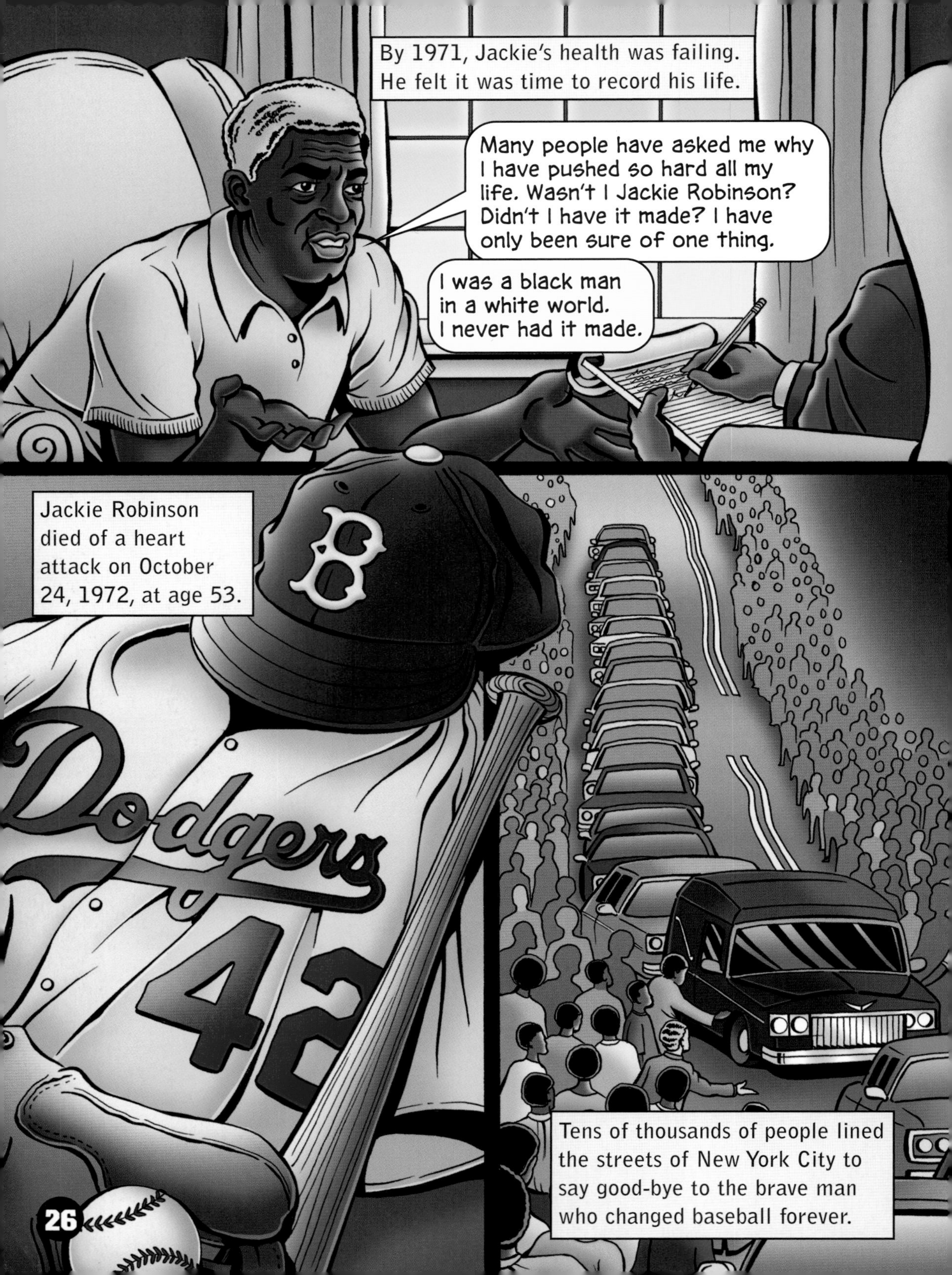
By 1971, Jackie's health was failing. He felt it was time to record his life.
Many people have asked me why I have pushed so hard all my life. Wasn't I Jackie Robinson? Didn't I have it made? I have only been sure of one thing.
I was a black man in a white world. I never had it made.
Jackie Robinson died of a heart attack on October 24, 1972, at age 53.
Dodgers
42
Tens of thousands of people lined the streets of New York City to say good-bye to the brave man who changed baseball forever.

JACKIE ROOSEVELT ROBINSON

BORN: January 31, 1919, Cairo, Georgia
HEIGHT: 5' 11" **WEIGHT:** 204 lbs
BATS: Right **THROWS:** Right

42

BROOKLYN DODGERS

Year	G	R	H	HR	RBI	SB	Avg
1947	151	125	175	12	48	29	.297
1948	147	108	170	12	85	22	.296
1949	156	122	203	16	124	37	.342
1950	144	99	170	14	81	12	.328
1951	153	106	185	19	88	25	.338
1952	149	104	157	19	75	24	.308
1953	136	109	159	12	95	17	.329
1954	124	62	120	15	59	7	.311
1955	105	51	81	8	36	12	.256
1956	117	61	98	10	43	12	.275
Career	1,382	947	1,518	137	734	197	.311

Jackie R. Robinson (signature)

KEY:
G = Games
R = Runs
H = Hits
HR = Home runs
RBI = Runs batted in
SB = Stolen bases
Avg = Batting average

More about JACKIE ROBINSON

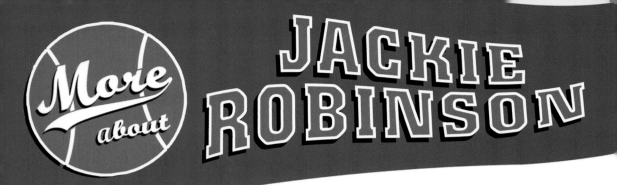

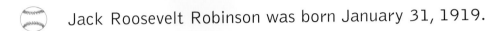

- Jack Roosevelt Robinson was born January 31, 1919.

- Jackie's middle name, Roosevelt, was given in honor of President Theodore Roosevelt. Roosevelt was against segregation. He died just before Jackie was born.

- A movie about Jackie, *The Jackie Robinson Story*, was made while he was still playing baseball. The movie studio needed a black actor who could run and hit well. Jackie ended up playing himself in the movie.

- Sometimes when Jackie was on base, a ball would get hit nearby that looked like it might result in a double play. Jackie would "accidentally" let the ball hit him as he ran between bases. This move would usually ruin the double play. The league saw this strategy as unfair, so it added a new rule. If a runner is struck by a hit ball, the runner and the batter are both out. This rule is sometimes called the "Jackie Robinson rule."

- In 1957, the new owner of the Brooklyn Dodgers moved the team to Los Angeles, California.

- Jackie was crucial to the integration of pro sports, but he was not the first black man to play pro baseball. Moses Fleetwood Walker played catcher for the American Association in 1884.

- Jackie excelled at every sport he ever played except one. While vacationing in the Catskill Mountains in New York, Jackie tried skiing. He fell down several times and gave up on skiing forever.

- Jackie and Rachel had three children: Jackie Jr., Sharon, and David. In 1971, Jackie Jr. was killed in a car accident at age 24, a little more than one year before Jackie died.

- To honor a former player, baseball teams sometimes retire a player's number. That number will never be worn by another player of the team. In 1997, Jackie's number 42 was retired from all of Major League Baseball.

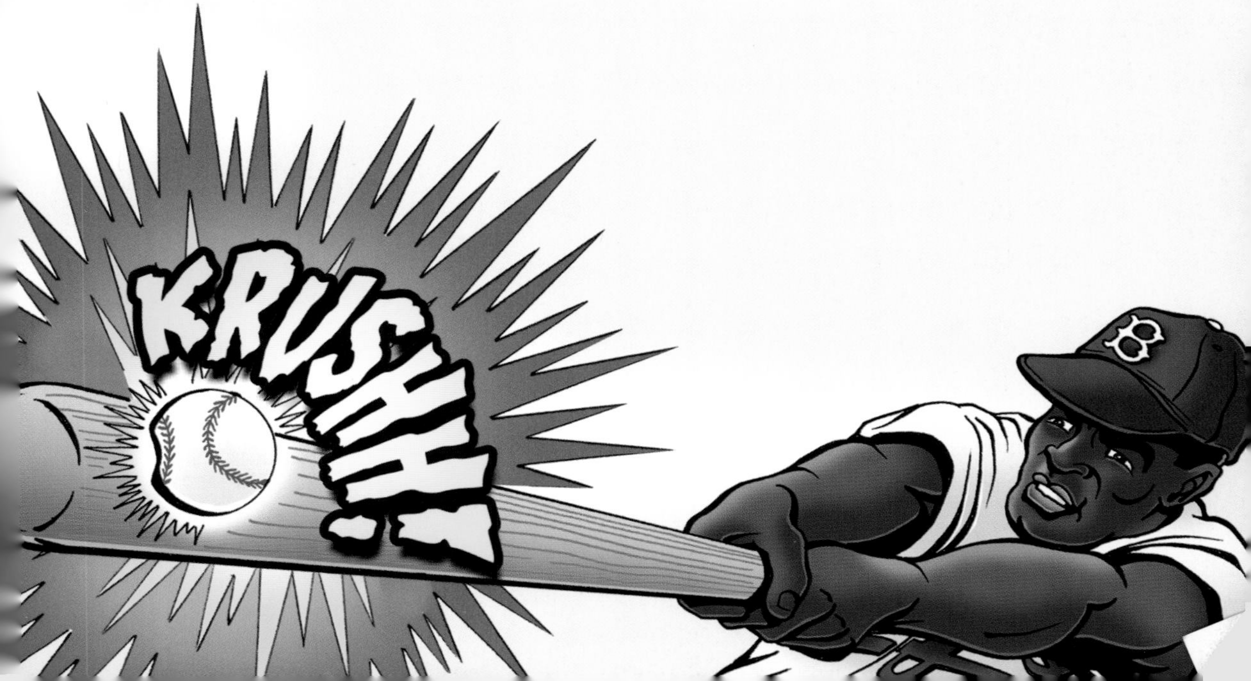
KRUSH!

GLOSSARY

court-martial (KORT-mar-shuhl)—to send someone to a military trial

draft (DRAFT)—to require to enlist in the military

morale (muh-RAL)—a person or group's feelings or state of mind

regulations (reg-yuh-LAY-shuhns)—official rules

reverend (REV-ruhnd)—the leader of a church

segregation (seg-ruh-GAY-shuhn)—the act of keeping people or groups apart

sharecropper (SHAIR-krop-ur)—a person who works farm fields for an owner in exchange for a small part of the profits

vandalize (VAN-duhl-ize)—to needlessly damage property

INTERNET SITES

FactHound offers a safe, fun way to find Internet sites related to this book. All of the sites on FactHound have been researched by our staff.

Here's how:

1. *Visit www.facthound.com*
2. Type in this special code **0736846336** for age-appropriate sites. Or enter a search word related to this book for a more general search.
3. Click on the **Fetch It** button.

FactHound will fetch the best sites for you!

READ MORE

De Marco, Tony. *Jackie Robinson.* Chanhassen, Minn.: Child's World, 2002.

Editors of *Time for Kids*, with Denise Lewis Patrick. *Jackie Robinson: Strong Inside and Out.* New York: HarperCollins, 2005.

Robinson, Sharon. *Promises to Keep: How Jackie Robinson Changed America.* New York: Scholastic, 2004.

Wheeler, Jill C. *Jackie Robinson.* Breaking Barriers. Edina, Minn.: Abdo, 2003.

BIBLIOGRAPHY

baseball-reference.com. Jackie Robinson. http://www.baseball-reference.com/r/robinja02.shtml.

Falkner, David. *Great Time Coming.* New York: Simon and Schuster, 1995.

Rampersad, Arnold. *Jackie Robinson.* New York: Knopf, 1997.

Robinson, Jackie. *I Never Had It Made.* New York: HarperCollins, 1995.

Robinson, Sharon. *Stealing Home: an Intimate Family Portrait by the Daughter of Jackie Robinson.* New York: HarperCollins, 1997.

Rowan, Carl T., with Jackie Robinson. *Wait Till Next Year: The Life Story of Jackie Robinson.* New York: Random House, 1960.

INDEX